101 Hands-On SCIENCE
EXPERIMENTS

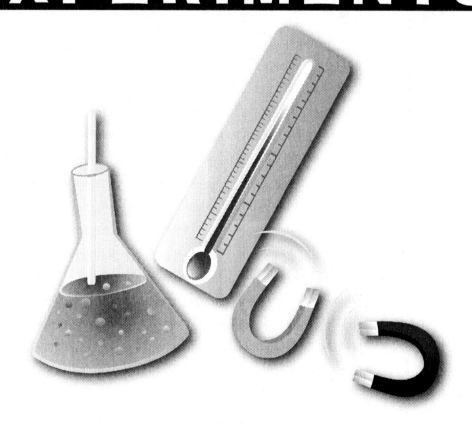

Phil Parratore

PRUFROCK PRESS INC.
WACO, TEXAS

Library of Congress Cataloging-in-Publication Data

Parratore, Phil.
  101 hands-on science experiments / by Phil Parratore.
    p. cm.
  ISBN-13: 978-1-59363-317-2 (pbk.)
  ISBN-10: 1-59363-317-3 (pbk.)
  1. Science—Experiments—Juvenile literature. I. Title. II. Title: One hundred one hands-on science experiments.
  Q182.3.P37 2008
  507.8—dc22
                         2008008123

Edited by Gretchen Sparling
Production Design by Marjorie Parker

ISBN-13: 978-1-59363-317-2
ISBN-10: 1-59363-317-3

At the time of this book's publication, all facts and figures cited are the most current available; all telephone numbers, addresses, and Web site URLs are accurate and active; all publications, organizations, Web sites, and other resources exist as described in this book; and all have been verified. The authors and Prufrock Press make no warranty or guarantee concerning the information and materials given out by organizations or content found at Web sites, and we are not responsible for any changes that occur after this book's publication. If you find an error or believe that a resource listed here is not as described, please contact Prufrock Press.

Prufrock Press Inc.
P.O. Box 8813
Waco, TX 76714-8813
Phone: (800) 998-2208
Fax: (800) 240-0333
http://www.prufrock.com

Dedication
This book is dedicated to my wonderful wife of 35 years, Karen, and my three beautiful children, Scott, Kurt, and Stacy.

Contents

Acknowledgements   ix

Introduction   1

Observation Report   6

Evaluation Rubric   7

Fire in the Hole   9

Wild and Crazy Reactions   23

Motion and Force, of Course   33

The Pressure Is On   45

Hot and Cold Stuff   59

In Living Color   73

Our Good Green Earth   85

Creepy Crawlers   99

Kitchen Science   111

About the Author   123

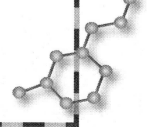

Acknowledgements

A warm and gracious thank you to the thousands of my math and science students—from elementary school children to adults—who have inspired me to keep my hands-on science ideas moving forward.

Introduction

Do you find yourself looking for new ideas to get your students motivated about science lessons? If you want to get your students excited about science concepts, the activities need to be simple, easy to understand, inexpensive to perform, and have a high "wow" factor. The experiments and demonstrations in *101 Hands-On Science Experiments* will engage students in your science curriculum, and make them eager for your next classroom experimentation. *101 Hands-On Science Experiments* includes the following topics of experimentation:

- **Fire in the Hole:** In this first section, your students will really "warm-up" to the fact that they are enthusiastically learning about heat energy and combustion in a unique and creative way.
- **Wild and Crazy Reactions:** Students will love participating or observing these fun, everyday chemical reactions that will have them wanting more.
- **Motion and Force, of Course:** Students will explore the forces defined by Newton's laws of motion by experimenting with magnetic force, air pressure, and the powerful display of rocket propulsion (and much more!).
- **The Pressure Is On:** You can't see pressure, but it's there! Air and water pressure have never been so easy to visualize and understand as in the experiments presented in this section.

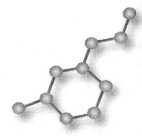

- **Hot and Cold Stuff:** When we use the terms *hot* and *cold*, exactly what do we mean? In this section, you and your students will explore temperature in an "absolute"-ly new way.
- **In Living Color:** Color is a concept that most of us don't really think about very often. This section is intended to take an in-depth look at the spectacular colors that surround us in our everyday lives.
- **Our Good Green Earth:** When you gaze at a plant, what exactly do you observe? Here your students have a chance to scrutinize plant science.
- **Creepy Crawlers:** Many people scream when they see tiny little critters from our natural world abound. But, fear not! Improve your "bug comfort zone" with the stimulating activities in this section.
- **Kitchen Science:** Have you ever thought of science in the kitchen? In this section you will turn your kitchen into one gigantic science lab. Students will be enthralled by these engaging activities that they can repeat at home (with a little help from parents).

How to Use This Book

The experiments in this book are useful in a classroom setting, or teachers also may want to recommend them for students to perform at home—allowing parents to interact with their children about concepts they are learning at school. This book also may be utilized in a homeschool setting, or by parents who are seeking to engage their children in educational activities outside of the classroom.

This book contains 101 fun, exciting, and ready-to-use active learning experiments that can be implemented immediately into your daily science lessons. Each individual activity is broken down into several subsections. They are as follows:

- **Purpose:** states the scientific objective of the activity.
- **Curriculum:** states which specific science lesson the experiment demonstrates.
- **Requirements:** offers two key elements of information:
  - *Time:* estimates how much time is required to complete the activity. Set up time is not included.
  - *Difficulty Level:* estimates the difficulty level of each activity from 1 (easy) to 4 (more complex).
- **Materials:** lists all of the materials you will need to complete the experiment. Most items used can be found around the house or at your local supermarket and hardware store.
- **Directions:** lists a step-by-step approach of exactly how to demonstrate the activity. Do not skip or substitute steps. When safety is a factor, *Safety Notes* will make you aware of any possible hazards, or denote if the experiments are recommended only for teacher demonstration.
- **Explanation:** discusses what happened in the experiment and how the results relate to the objective, and/or the curriculum.
- **Variation:** offers an interesting extension for selected activities.

Grade Levels

All of the activities in *101 Hands-On Science Experiments* are effective at the elementary level, but they easily can be adapted for secondary learners. One of the most exciting groups of students that I work with is the gifted and talented population. Their ability to extrapolate information and apply it to the real world is truly remarkable. The gifted child not only wants to be challenged, he or she *needs* to be challenged. What better way to tap the creative juices of the gifted child than the interactive methodology of hands-on science experiments, particularly when they are simple, enjoyable, and easy-to-repeat at home or at school. For the secondary-level student, a demonstration can sometimes drive home the understanding of a complex science concept taught in advanced science courses.

Standards and Curriculum Integration

101 Hands-On Science Experiments bridges the gap between mandated and creative curriculum, by working within and exemplifying state and national science education and gifted education standards.

Hands-on learning is active learning for the gifted child. The research in support of active learning is overwhelming. Interactive learning operates at many levels in a challenging classroom because it gives students a chance to do something that produces immediate results during your science lesson. By using the activities in this book, teachers can plan science lessons that engage a student's thinking processes in learning and applying scientific knowledge. The National Science Education Standards detail the use of hands-on learning in today's science classrooms. The standards include eight categories of content that should be present in a quality science education curriculum:

- unifying concepts and processes in science,
- science as inquiry,
- physical science,
- life science,
- earth and space science,
- science and technology,
- science in personal and social perspectives, and
- history and nature of science.

To read more about the Science Content Standards in detail, please visit http://books.nap.edu/openbook.php??record_id=4962&page=1.

Your students will appreciate when you make a math or statistics lesson more hands-on by integrating your lessons together with a science experiment. You can do this by requiring students to use the results of their own individual experiment, and combine the data with several other classmates'. Then, have your students graph the results by using several different types of graphs (e.g., line, pie, bar). The act of recording and organizing data has multiple benefits for the creative learner that will address the visual, logical, goal-oriented learning that will benefit students' day-to-day lives.

Evaluation

Teachers have several options for the evaluation of students' performance in hands-on science demonstrations. The first option this book provides is the Observation Report on p. 6. This report may be reproduced and distributed for students to fill out during the postexperiment classroom discussion (teachers also may post these questions and require students to answer on their own paper).

The second evaluation option provided by this book is the Evaluation Rubric on p. 7. To use this rating system, circle the number that best reflects student performance of the goals or objectives listed on the rubric. This evaluation may be of students' Observation Report, or of a student-performed demonstration. You may use this rubric at your discretion and adapt your grading method and procedures to your individual classroom.

Beyond the Classroom

Many educators know from experience that student learning is extended and reinforced when real-world scenarios are brought into the classroom for students to explore. The following are suggestions for extending your students' hands-on science learning beyond regular classroom instruction:

- Have students perform some of their favorite experiments or hands-on activities in front of their classmates or other students. Set up booths in the classroom where students can perform selected science experiments and demonstrate some of the scientific concepts listed in this book. Invite other visitors, such as other classes or family members, to visit your class and witness these student demonstrations.
- You may even want to go as far as organizing a schoolwide science fair at your school, utilizing the experiments provided in this book.
- Contact local industrial businesses and environmental groups, and invite a spokesperson—such as an engineer, technician, or scientist—to discuss how science affects daily life in the community. Many companies and organizations welcome opportunities to get involved with schools. Your local chamber of commerce may be able to assist you with this task.
- Because real-world science applications and career education are such important components of a well-rounded education, consider arranging a field trip for your class to tour a local factory, scientific institution, or public utility plant or office. To go above and beyond, arrange personal meetings for selected student groups to interview plant managers, research scientists, engineers, and maintenance or office staff from a local company. Students may then write up their interviews for publication in a class newsletter, or they may give in-class presentations about their experiences.

Let the Experiments Begin!

One final thought before the scientific gratification begins—I strongly encourage you to use the activities in this book as a catalyst for developing your own scientific projects and use them to enhance your students' vigorous learning process. Hands-on education works in the gifted classroom because it is student-centered, interactive learning. As your students practice the freedom to gather information and organize it themselves, they also experience the excitement and pure raw power of becoming accomplished, proficient learners.

Name:_____ Date:_____

Observation Report

Observation is a very important part of the scientific inquiry method. For each hands-on science experiment that you observe or demonstrate on your own, answer the questions below.

Name of Science Activity:_____

What did you observe?

_____

_____

_____

How do you explain what you observed in this experiment?

_____

_____

_____

How does this experiment connect to other scientific facts that you already know?

_____

_____

_____

What questions do you have after witnessing/performing this experiment?

_____

_____

_____

Evaluation Rubric

Rating System: 1 = Poor   2 = Fair   3 = Good   4 = Excellent

Demonstrates understanding of scientific concepts.	1 2 3 4
Keeps accurate records of observations.	1 2 3 4
Organizes data/results through categorizing and ordering.	1 2 3 4
Draws logical conclusions from experimental results.	1 2 3 4
Effectively communicates scientific learning.	1 2 3 4
Makes connections to science across the curriculum.	1 2 3 4
Makes inferences.	1 2 3 4
Applies knowledge to solve problems.	1 2 3 4
Uses lab equipment and supplies appropriately (if applicable).	1 2 3 4
Demonstrates the scientific method.	1 2 3 4
Works cooperatively with others.	1 2 3 4
Completes assignments on time.	1 2 3 4

Teacher Comments:

_____

_____

_____

_____

_____

_____

Fire in the Hole

From the beginning of time, the human race has always been fascinated by fire. Whether it's rubbing two sticks together or illuminating the sky with Fourth-of-July fireworks, flames and fire are great forms of entertainment and education. In your science classroom, there is nothing more exciting or motivating for your students than to observe science activities and experiments that involve fire. Your students, as well as your colleagues and administrators, will be highly impressed when they see an open flame in a controlled environment. As with any science laboratory, safety is of the utmost importance when working with an open flame. Caution is advised. These experiments are intended for teacher or adult demonstration. (Some are student-friendly, but adult supervision is strongly suggested.) The use of a long-tipped butane lighter is highly advised.

CANDLE RACE 10
IT'S SO A-PEELING 11
IT'S WINDY IN HERE! 12
POP DU-WOPS 13
ASHES TO ASHES 14
BANANA, FANNA' FOE 15
INSULATING CUP 16
YOU LIGHT UP MY LIFE 17
BALANCING CANDLES 18
BYE, BYE, MS. AMERICAN PIE 19
MONEY TO BURN 20
FOUNTAINS OF YOUTH 21
OXYGEN EATERS 22

CANDLE RACE

Purpose
To illustrate how and why fire needs oxygen to burn.

Curriculum
Chemical reactions

Requirements
Time: 5 minutes   *Difficulty Level:* 1

Materials
- three identical candles and holders
- medium-sized empty glass
- large-sized empty glass
- matches

Directions
1. Light the three candles.
2. Place the different-sized jars over two of the candles at the same time.
3. Observe which candle is the first to extinguish.
4. Explain the requirements of combustion to students.

Safety Note: Use caution when working with burning candles.

Explanation
Combustion requires oxygen to burn. The candle with an unlimited air supply will burn for a long time. The candle in the large glass has more air; therefore, it will burn longer than the candle in the smaller-sized glass. These two candles will extinguish because there is no oxygen remaining in the jars to support the combustion reaction.

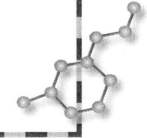

Fire in the Hole

IT'S SO A-PEELING

Purpose

To display the flammability of lemon oil.

Curriculum

Surface area and combustion

Requirements

Time: 5 minutes   *Difficulty Level:* 1

Materials

- a candle
- lemon
- match
- knife

Directions

1. Stand the candle securely on a flat surface that is visible to students.
2. Cut or peel a large chunk of lemon peel.
3. Light the candle.
4. Quickly and firmly squeeze the lemon peel near the candle's flame, spraying juice onto the flame.
5. Allow students to observe the reaction by performing this action several times.
6. Explain which elements of the lemon juice are combusting and evaporating.

Safety Note: Use caution when working with the knife and open flame.

Explanation

As the lemon peel is squeezed, its juice squirts onto the candle's flame. This juice contains oil and water—the oil burns as it passes through the flame, and the water evaporates. This causes a sparkle of fireworks when the lemon's oil is ignited by the flame. The oil provides for the combustion element of this experiment, while the water is evaporated.

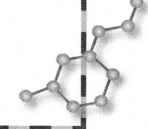

IT'S WINDY IN HERE!

Fire in the Hole

Purpose

To illustrate differences in air pressure caused by moving air.

Curriculum

Air pressure

Requirements

Time: 2 minutes   *Difficulty Level:* 1

Materials

- a candle
- funnel
- matches

Directions

1. Light the candle and set it on a sturdy table.
2. Put the spout of the funnel in your mouth.
3. Within a few inches of the flame, blow air onto the candle through the funnel.
4. Then, reverse the funnel and blow air at the flame.
5. Repeat this process, relighting the candle as needed.
6. Explain the differences in air pressure that are being illustrated by the funnel.

Safety Note: Use caution when working with a lit candle.

Explanation

Your candle should remain lit as air rushes through the funnel and slows down, reducing the air pressure. The air in the funnel is filled by the room's air pressure. So, the air you blow into the smaller filter of the funnel travels along the walls of the funnel, missing the flame. The differences in air pressure guide the path of the air. Reversing the funnel and blowing air through the filter hole should blow out the candle because the air is compressed into a thin stream that focuses on the flame.

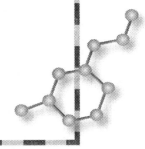

POP DU-WOPS

Purpose

To show that carbon dioxide gas will not support an open flame.

Curriculum

Chemical reactions

Requirements

Time: 2 minutes   *Difficulty Level:* 1

Materials

- bottle or can of a carbonated beverage (any flavor)
- glass
- matches

Directions

1. Pour the carbonated beverage into the glass.
2. Carefully light the match and place it over the glass.
3. Repeat this action several times to demonstrate that the match will extinguish when placed over the bubbling carbonated liquid.

Safety Note: Use caution when lighting matches; wear safety goggles. This experiment is only recommended for teacher or adult demonstration.

Explanation

The match is quickly extinguished when you hold it over the bubbling beverage because the liquid is emitting carbon dioxide gas. This gas is under a fair amount of pressure, so when the drink container is opened the bubbles of gas burst at the surface. The area directly above the glass becomes full of carbon dioxide. When placed over the glass, the match quickly burns up whatever oxygen is in the immediate area, and is left only to burn the carbon dioxide. Combustion requires oxygen.

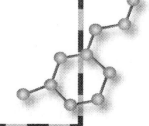

ASHES TO ASHES

Purpose

To exhibit how catalysts works.

Curriculum

Surface area and chemical reactions

Requirements

Time: 5 minutes   *Difficulty Level*: 2

Materials

- sugar cube
- pie or tin pan
- fireplace or charcoal ash
- long-tipped butane lighter

Directions

1. Place a sugar cube in a tin pan and try to set it on fire.
2. When this attempt is unsuccessful (or requires holding the flame to the cube for a long amount of time), dab the corner of the cube with a trace of ash.
3. The ash serves as a catalyst to igniting the sugar cube. Explain the role of catalysts to students.

Safety Note: Use caution when working with an open flame and flammable material. Always wear safety glasses and tie long hair back when working with an open flame. Roll back long sleeves.

Explanation

The sugar will burn with a blue flame until it is completely gone. The ash cannot be lighted separately, but the ash initiates the combustion of the sugar. A substance that brings about a chemical reaction, without itself being changed, is called a catalyst. The ash acts as a catalyst when sprinkled onto the sugar cube. A catalyst is a substance that speeds up a chemical reaction without undergoing any chemical change itself. The sugar cube will burn with a blue flame until it is completely gone.

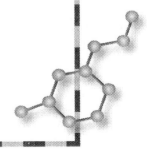

BANANA, FANNA' FOE

Purpose
To demonstrate the chemical process of burning.

Curriculum
Chemical and heat reactions

Requirements
Time: 1 minute   *Difficulty Level:* 2

Materials
- knife
- banana
- almond or pecan (cut in a sliver shaped like the narrowed piece of a candlewick)
- matches or a lighter

Directions
1. Using the knife, shape the banana to resemble a candle.
2. Place the almond or pecan in the top of the banana, resembling a candlewick.
3. Ignite the nut (this may take a few tries).
4. Let the "candle" burn for a few moments.
5. Blow out the "candle" and explain to students the chemical reaction that is taking place while the nut is burning.

Safety Note: As with anything flammable, caution is advised. Wear safety goggles. This experiment is only recommended for teacher or adult demonstration. Use caution with the knife.

Explanation
The nut burns because all nuts have very high oil content, and oil burns. Also, the black material on the nut is carbon. Carbon is one of the elements that make up all living creatures. Carbon is a by-product of the reaction.

Fire in the Hole

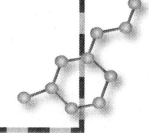

INSULATING CUP

Fire in the Hole

Purpose

To display the insulating value of a paper cup.

Curriculum

Insulation

Requirements

Time: 5 minutes   *Difficulty Level*: 2

Materials

- paper cup
- long-tipped butane lighter
- $\frac{1}{2}$ cup of water

Directions

1. Fill the paper cup with $\frac{1}{2}$ cup of water.
2. Carefully hold an open flame directly under the cup for a few minutes. Don't touch the flame to the cup.
3. Remove the lighter from the cup.
4. Place your finger in the water and note the temperature of the water.
5. Explain why the paper is a good insulator to the water, allowing the water to heat up quickly.

Safety Note: Make sure the flame is directly under the cup of water. You may hold the cup with your other hand, but make sure you do not burn your fingers on the flame.

Explanation

The cup should not burn (don't touch the flame to the cup). Paper is a good thermal insulator; therefore, the heat from the flame is transferred directly to the water, not the paper. If you hold an open flame under the cup long enough the water will actually start to boil.

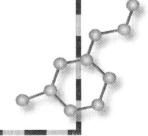

YOU LIGHT UP MY LIFE

Purpose
To demonstrate the combustibility of vapors.

Curriculum
Vaporization

Requirements
Time: 1 minute   *Difficulty Level*: 2

Materials
- candle with a large wick
- wooden safety matches

Directions
1. Light the candle in a safe place and allow it to burn for a few seconds.
2. Light another match and blow out the candle.
3. Place the lit match over the candle's wick into the white smoke. Do not touch the wick with the flame.
4. You may demonstrate this several times to ensure that all students can see that the candle lights without touching the match to the wick.

Safety Note: Wear safety goggles and be cautious with the lit flame.

Explanation
The candle will relight without the match touching the wick. After the flame is blown out, a vapor, or gas, is produced as evident by the smoke. This vapor comes from a chemical in the wax called *stearin*. Stearin stays hot enough after the flame is blown out that it continues to evaporate into the air and produce a vapor. Because this vapor is combustible, it can easily relight.

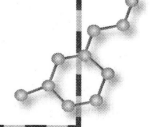

BALANCING CANDLES

Purpose

To display a balancing act with two flames on a single candle.

Curriculum

Newton's Third Law of Motion

Requirements

Time: 5 minutes   *Difficulty Level:* 3

Materials

- long round candle
- round toothpicks
- two glasses of the same size
- matches or a lighter
- knife
- aluminum foil

Directions

1. Prepare the candle so it may be lighted at both ends by scraping the wax off the bottom end and exposing the wick. You may have to burn the wick to remove the wax.
2. Stick round toothpicks on opposite sides (not ends) of the candle. Then, balance the toothpicks between two glasses, slightly tilting one side of the candle toward the table. You may have to adjust the toothpicks until the candle will properly tilt toward the table.
3. Place your glass-and-candle combination in the center of a sheet of foil.
4. Light both ends of the candle and allow students to observe for a few minutes.
5. Explain the reactions taking place, and how Newton's Third Law of Motion applies to this demonstration.

Explanation

When the candle is lighted at both ends, the end tilting downward will burn more wax and become lighter. After it tilts up, the angle of the lower candle end will then burn more wax—causing the candle to rock back and forth, often quite vigorously. Newton's Third Law of Motion states that for every action there is an equal and opposite reaction.

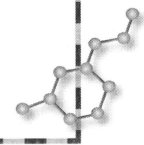

BYE, BYE, MS. AMERICAN PIE

Purpose

To illustrate how oxygen is needed to support combustion. Also, to display how combustion impacts air and water pressure.

Curriculum

Combustion; air and water pressure

Requirements

Time: 5 minutes   *Difficulty Level:* 3

Materials

- wax candle about 2 inches tall and 1–2 inches wide
- pie tin with no holes in the bottom
- large-mouthed glass jar
- water
- matches
- food coloring (optional)

Directions

1. Fill the pie tin about half full of water. Stir in the optional food coloring.
2. Place the candle in the center of the tin and (after making sure it is sturdy) light the candle.
3. Invert the jar and place it over the candle.
4. Allow the candle to burn underneath the jar and observe.
5. Explain to students why the candle goes out, and also note the rise in the water inside the glass jar.

Safety Note: Use caution: If the candle starts to float when you add the water to the tin, pour out the water, light the candle and melt a few drops of hot wax in the middle of the tin and stick the candle on the hot wax to hold the candle in place.

Explanation

When the candle goes out due to the lack of oxygen, there is less air in the jar, therefore there's less pressure. The higher pressurized air on the outside of the jar pushes the water from the plate into the jar, causing the water inside the jar to rise.

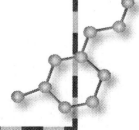

MONEY TO BURN

Purpose
To demonstrate the flammability of alcohol.

Curriculum
Combustion and density

Requirements
Time: 2 minutes   *Difficulty Level*: 3

Materials
- 1 cup of rubbing alcohol
- $1 bill
- medium-size container
- tweezers
- water
- long-tipped butane lighter

Directions
1. Mix 1 cup of rubbing alcohol with 1 cup of water. Stir well.
2. Using the tweezers, dip the entire bill in the mixture. Let it sit in the liquid for a few seconds.
3. While carefully holding the bill with the tweezers, light the bill with the lighter. (Keep the jar of alcohol far away from the open flame.)
4. Allow the money to "burn" for about 5–8 seconds. (Extinguish the flame should you see any of the paper ignite.)
5. Explain how the alcohol coats the money and allows the paper to appear to be on fire, while it's only the liquid burning off the dollar bill.

Safety Note: Use caution and wear safety goggles. This experiment is only recommended for teacher or adult demonstration.

Explanation
The alcohol forms a thin coating on the dollar bill. Because alcohol is flammable, and less dense than the water, it stays on top of the money and it burns very rapidly. The bill should not burn because the alcohol will not rapidly absorb into the tight, woven fibers of the money. Regular paper will not work because the alcohol is more rapidly absorbed into more loosely knit fibers.

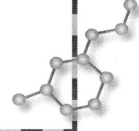

Fire in the Hole

FOUNTAINS OF YOUTH

Purpose

To identify the reactions of hot and cold gases.

Curriculum

Water pressure

Requirements

Time: 20 minutes   *Difficulty Level:* 4

Materials

- small jar with a screw-on lid
- plastic straw
- match
- large, empty coffee can
- scissors
- hammer and thick nail
- long candle
- hot tap water
- tray of ice cubes

Fire in the Hole

Directions

1. Use the hammer and nail to make a hole in the center of the jar's lid. The hole should be large enough to fit the straw through.
2. Cut the straw in half and push one piece halfway through the hole in the lid.
3. Let the candle burn until the wax on top begins to melt. Drip some hot wax around the edge of the hole to seal the straw in the lid.
4. Fill the coffee can ¾ full with water and ice cubes.
5. In order to warm up the jar, carefully hold it in the hot water for about one minute.
6. Quickly screw the lid on the jar and place it into the can of ice.
7. Observe the water shoot out of the straw. Explain the properties of water and air pressure and how they apply to this demonstration.

Safety Note: Use caution when working with the hammer, matches, scissors, and the hot wax from the candle.

Explanation

Water and air cannot occupy the same space at the same time. Hot air needs more space than an equal amount of cold air. When gases (such as the gases in air) are heated, they expand. When you put the jar into the cold water, the air in the jar cooled very quickly and began to contract, thus reducing the air pressure. The declining air pressure on the surface of the cold water in the can then pushed the cold water up the straw and into the jug.

OXYGEN EATERS

Fire in the Hole

Purpose

To demonstrate how the decomposition of products produces oxygen gas.

Curriculum

Chemical change

Requirements

Time: 5 minutes   *Difficulty Level:* 4

Materials

- bottle of 3-percent hydrogen peroxide
- package of fresh, dry yeast
- jar or container
- wood splint
- long-tipped butane lighter

Directions

1. Place a few ounces of hydrogen peroxide in the jar or container.
2. Sprinkle some yeast in the jar and mix.
3. Make a glowing splint by lighting the tip of the splint with the lighter and then blow out the flame. There should be a red glow at the end of the wooden stick.
4. Place the glowing splint into the mouth of the jar, near the surface of the bubbling hydrogen peroxide. The flame should relight.
5. Explain the chemical reaction taking place at the surface of the hydrogen peroxide.

Safety Note: Caution is advised. Wear safety goggles. This experiment is only recommended for teacher or adult demonstration.

Explanation

The chemical reaction between the yeast and the hydrogen peroxide is called a decomposition, or reaction. The yeast caused the hydrogen peroxide to release oxygen molecules above the surface. Because oxygen is flammable, it caused the glowing splint to relight.

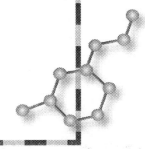

Wild and Crazy Reactions

Ask your students if they have ever seen rust on a car or fence. Explain to them that not long before, these metal objects glistened in the sun. But, something happened to these metal pieces that left them with a reddish-brown rust color and flaky appearance. Describe to students how rusting (or oxidation) is just one of many kinds of chemical changes that go on around us every day. A hamburger being cooked on the grill, flowers growing and blooming, calories burning in the human body, or, likewise, gasoline burning in a car's engine are all actions during which properties are changing. These changes are essentially chemical reactions. In the activities in this section, you and your students will take a fun look at how certain actions cause everyday chemical reactions.

CHALK IT UP 24
HAUNTED BOTTLE. 25
BOUNCING POPCORN. 26
JACK FROST'S SECRET MESSAGE 27
OL' RUSTY 28
THE CHEM-MYSTERY OF FLOATING MOTH BALLS 29
ERUPTING VOLCANIC. 30
MISTY SMOKE RINGS 31
DON'T HOLD YOUR BREATH. 32

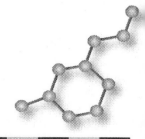

CHALK IT UP

Purpose

To simulate the effect of acid rain on buildings.

Curriculum

Acid rain and chemical change

Requirements

Time: 1 minute   *Difficulty Level*: 1

Materials

- two clear glasses or cups
- two pieces of chalk
- vinegar
- water

Directions

1. Fill one glass ¾ full of vinegar.
2. Fill the other glass ¾ full of water.
3. Place a piece of chalk in each glass.
4. Observe and note the difference in reaction.

Explanation

While in the vinegar, the chalk will begin to produce a gas, which you will see as bubbles. The chalk in the water will not bubble. Vinegar is acetic acid, and chalk simulates a mineral called limestone. Limestone is used in the construction of many buildings. Excess acid in our environment, in the form of acid rain, will eat away at limestone over many years in much the same way the vinegar eats away the chalk.

Variation

Even though the reaction takes place immediately, keep the chalk in the vinegar overnight, and then observe what happens. Or, try squirting lemon or grapefruit juice (citric acid) onto a piece of chalk and observe the bubbly reaction.

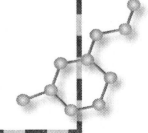

HAUNTED BOTTLE

Purpose

To demonstrate the thermal expansion of gases.

Curriculum

Gas formation and temperature changes

Requirements

Time: 3 minutes (plus freezing *Time*)   *Difficulty Level*: 1

Materials

- 12–16-ounce empty and uncapped glass soda bottle
- a nickel coin
- freezer
- several drops of water
- a table

Directions

1. Place the empty, uncapped bottle in the freezer for about 15–20 minutes.
2. Remove the bottle and quickly place it on the table in front of you.
3. Quickly moisten the opening of the bottle and put the nickel on top of it.
4. Cup your hands around the bottle for one to two minutes. Do not move or shake the bottle.
5. Observe what the nickel does and discuss with students.

Explanation

The nickel will pop up and down a few times, making a clanking sound. By putting the bottle in the freezer, you are cooling the air inside. Your warm hand reheats the air in the bottle, which causes the air inside to expand. Thermal expansion is when air takes up more space when heated. The nickel acts as a one-way valve. The reheated air breaks the seal by pushing the nickel up, allowing the air to escape. This causes the nickel to pop up and down, making the bottle act as if it were haunted.

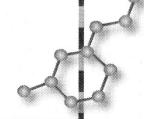

Wild and Crazy Reactions

BOUNCING POPCORN

Purpose

To show a chemical reaction involving common household products.

Curriculum

Acids and bases; gas formations

Requirements

Time: 5 minutes   *Difficulty Level:* 2

Materials

- water
- clear glass or cup
- vinegar
- baking soda
- toothpicks
- uncooked popcorn kernels
- a spoon

Directions

1. Fill the cup half full of water, and then add 2 ounces of vinegar.
2. Add a pinch of baking soda and stir.
3. Add a few kernels of popcorn to the mixture (these will sink to the bottom of the glass).
4. Add a few more pinches of the baking soda.
5. Using the toothpick, poke at the bubbles forming around the popcorn kernels (which have now risen to the surface of the water/vinegar solution). Then, observe the popcorn kernels as they sink.
6. Explain to students why this chemical reaction between baking soda and vinegar is taking place, and what this means for the kernel of popcorn.

Explanation

The chemical reaction between baking soda and vinegar produces a gas called carbon dioxide. Carbon dioxide is an invisible gas, but in this experiment you actually can see the carbon dioxide in the form of bubbles. These bubbles, which are lighter than the water/vinegar solution, attach themselves to the popcorn kernels and cause the kernels to float to the top of the cup. When the bubbles hit the air they burst (or you can burst them with your toothpick), causing the kernels to drop back to the bottom of the cup.

JACK FROST'S SECRET MESSAGE

Purpose
To demonstrate the crystallization of salt.

Curriculum
Physical change and crystal formation

Requirements
Time: 10 minutes (plus drying *Time*)   *Difficulty Level:* 2

Materials
- 1½ cups of water
- 1½ cups of Epsom salt
- saucepan
- long-tipped cotton swabs
- dark-colored construction paper
- a heating source

Directions
1. Mix the water and the Epsom salt in the saucepan.
2. Heat the mixture until the salt is completely dissolved.
3. Let the mixture cool.
4. Dip the cotton swab into the mixture and write a message on the construction paper.
5. Set the paper aside to dry and watch your secret message appear.
6. Discuss this reaction with students.

Explanation
The salt will appear on your paper as frost-like white crystals. As the water evaporates, the salt is crystallized and outlines the words or drawings formed on the paper. The dark-colored paper will show the contrast much better than a light-colored paper. (Epsom salt is actually made from a chemical called magnesium sulfate.)

Wild and Crazy Reactions

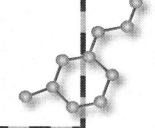

OL' RUSTY

Purpose

To demonstrate the chemical reaction that creates rust.

Curriculum

Oxidation and chemical change

Requirements

Time: 5 minutes   *Difficulty Level:* 2

Materials

- small piece of steel wool
- glass jar
- 4 tablespoons of liquid bleach
- 2 tablespoons of vinegar
- a spoon

Directions

1. Place the steel wool in the clean jar.
2. Add the bleach and vinegar.
3. Stir with a spoon for about 5 minutes.
4. Discuss the reaction that is taking place in the jar.

Safety Note: Use caution when working with bleach and do this activity with adequate ventilation. Wear safety goggles.

Explanation

The red powder you see at the bottom of the jar is rust—the chemical term for which is iron oxide. The chemical reaction that occurred between the bleach, vinegar, and iron in the steel wool is known as oxidation. Steel wool rusts because of the iron in the steel wool combining with oxygen. In chemistry a chemical reaction is defined as a process in which one or more substances are changed into new substances.

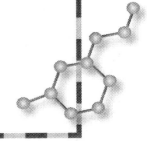

THE CHEM-MYSTERY OF FLOATING MOTH BALLS

Purpose

To demonstrate how the density of mothballs will change.

Curriculum

Density and chemical change

Requirements

Time: 10 minutes   *Difficulty Level:* 2

Materials

- 3 mothballs
- 1 tablespoon of vinegar
- 1 tablespoon of baking soda
- a glass of water

Directions

1. Add the vinegar and the baking soda to the glass of water.
2. Place the mothballs in the liquid and observe.
3. Discuss the change in the mothballs' density.

Safety Note: Wash hands thoroughly after handling mothballs. Do not ingest.

Explanation

At first, the mothballs sink because they are denser than water. The vinegar and baking soda combines chemically to make bubbles of carbon dioxide gas. The bubbles collect on the mothballs, causing them to float to the top. While the mothballs are floating at the top, some of the bubbles of gas burst into the air causing them to lose some of their buoyancy. This sinking and floating will continue until the vinegar and baking soda stop combining and producing carbon dioxide.

Wild and Crazy Reactions

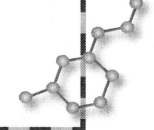

ERUPTING VOLCANIC

Purpose
To simulate a volcanic eruption using a chemical reaction.

Curriculum
Earth formations and chemical change

Requirements
Time: 10 minutes   *Difficulty Level:* 3

Materials
- baking soda
- spoon
- empty plastic soda bottle
- glass baking pan
- dry dirt
- 1 cup of vinegar
- red food coloring
- funnel
- topsoil

Directions
1. Place 2 tablespoons of baking soda into the bottle.
2. Place the soda bottle in the pan.
3. Shape dirt around the bottle to form a mountain. Do not cover the bottle's mouth and do not get dirt inside the bottle.
4. Color the vinegar with red food coloring, then using the funnel pour the liquid into the bottle.
5. Stand back and observe the reaction between the baking soda and the vinegar— this will force the mixture out of the bottle.

Safety Note: The reaction is a bit messy, so be mindful.

Explanation
A chemical reaction between the baking soda and the vinegar produces carbon dioxide gas. The gas builds up enough pressure to force the mixture out of the top of the bottle. In an active volcano, there is an opening (or rupture) in the surface (or crust) that allows hot, molten rock, ash, and gases to escape from below the surface. These escaping materials undergo a similar reaction to that of the baking soda and vinegar. Volcanic activity involving the extrusion of rock forms mountains and other land features over long periods of time.

MISTY SMOKE RINGS

Purpose

To demonstrate the characteristics of dry ice.

Curriculum

Temperature and phase change

Requirements

Time: 5 minutes   *Difficulty Level:* 3

Materials

- small piece of dry ice
- 12-ounce clear plastic cup
- piece of cardboard to fit on top of the cup
- scissors
- ice tongs
- water
- food coloring (optional)

Directions

1. Fill the cup halfway with water.
2. Add a drop or two of food coloring to the water for effect (optional).
3. Cut a round ½-inch hole in the center of the cardboard.
4. Using the ice tongs, place a marble-sized piece of dry ice in the cup.
5. Place the cardboard on top of the cup.
6. Gently squeeze the cup while holding the cardboard in place. Notice the misty smoke rings.
7. Explain why this reaction is taking place, and discuss the properties of dry ice.

Safety Note: Do not touch the dry ice with your hand.

Explanation

With practice, each squeeze of the cup can generate a smoke ring that follows a short trajectory path. This is due to the fairly high density of the carbon dioxide-filled mist. Dry ice is simply frozen carbon dioxide.

Wild and Crazy Reactions

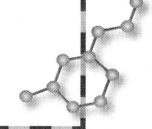

DON'T HOLD YOUR BREATH

Purpose

To demonstrate the presence of carbon dioxide in an exhaled breath.

Curriculum

Chemical change and reactions

Requirements

Time: 5 minutes (plus overnight for setup) *Difficulty Level:* 4

Materials

Part A:
- pickling lime (food-canning section of grocery store)
- two 1-quart glass jars with lids   • water
- a tablespoon

Part B:
- clear cup or glass   • straw

Directions

Part A: Making of Limewater
1. Fill one of the jars about ⅔ full of water.
2. Add 1 tablespoon of the pickling lime and stir.
3. Cap the jar and allow it to stand, undisturbed, overnight.
4. The next day, pour off the clear liquid into the second jar. The clear liquid in the second jar is an indicator called limewater. Be careful not to pour any of the settled powder into the second jar.

Part B: Testing Your Breath
1. Pour a few ounces of the limewater into the glass.
2. Place the straw at the bottom of the glass and slowly exhale into the limewater. Keep blowing into the straw until the liquid changes colors.
3. Discuss why this causes the water to become milky-looking.

Safety Note: Caution students not to inhale from the straw and drink the limewater. Although it isn't poisonous, the taste of limewater is unpleasant.

Explanation

The liquid is a solution called limewater, which is a compound that consists of water and calcium atoms. Limewater is a chemical indicator that detects the presence of carbon dioxide gas. A chemical reaction occurs when carbon dioxide molecules (the gas we exhale after each breath) mixes with the limewater. This causes the water to appear milky.

Motion and Force, of Course

Explain to students that the relationship between force and motion, commonly know as a push or pull, was expressed by Sir Isaac Newton in his three laws of motion: (1) If no force acts on a body in motion, it will continue to move uniformly in a straight line; (2) if force acts on a body, the body will produce a change of motion proportionate to the force, and in the same direction (as that in which the force acts); and (3) for every action, there is an equal and opposite reaction. Newton's laws of motion, together with his law of gravity, provide a basic explanation of motion of everyday objects under everyday conditions. Point out to students that the next time they see someone pushing a shopping cart, driving in a car, or even walking, they are witnessing Newton's laws of motion—laws they will learn much more about in these teacher-demonstrated experiments.

HAVE A BALL 34

HELIUM ICE CUBE 35

AN ACTION REACTION 36

DUELING BALLOONS 37

INDY 500 38

WATER/AIR BALLOON 39

I'M ATTRACTED TO YOU 40

JET ENGINE BALLOON 41

WACKY SPACE SHUTTLE 42

BUTTON YOUR FLY-WHEEL 43

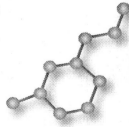

HAVE A BALL

Purpose
To illustrate how potential energy converts to kinetic energy.

Curriculum
Transfer of energy

Requirements
Time: 1 minute   *Difficulty Level:* 1

Materials
- tennis ball
- volleyball

Directions
1. Drop the tennis ball to the floor from shoulder height.
2. Do the same with the volleyball.
3. Now, place the tennis ball on top of the volleyball and drop both simultaneously.
4. Discuss the results as a class.

Explanation
The tennis ball rebounds much higher when dropped with the volleyball, because the volleyball has already hit the floor first and is moving back up by the time it hits the tennis ball. This is an example of the transfer of potential energy (stationary energy) to kinetic energy (motion energy), as well as an example of Newton's Second Law that states that if force acts on a body, the body will produce a change of motion proportionate to the force, and in the same direction.

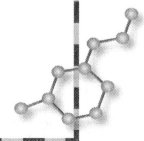

Motion and Force

HELIUM ICE CUBE

Purpose

To compare how forces and motion of cold air and warm air interact with molecules within a polymer.

Curriculum

Temperature changes

Requirements

Time: 5 minutes   *Difficulty Level:* 1

Materials

- one helium-filled latex balloon
- a freezer

Directions

1. Place the balloon in the freezer (or take it outside on a very cold day—under 30 degrees Fahrenheit) for about 5 minutes.
2. Take the balloon out of the freezer and bring it back into the room.
3. Discuss your observations.

Explanation

When the balloon is put in the freezer, the heavier, cold air forces the motion of these molecules to be trapped inside the balloon, which in turn slows them down. Therefore, the balloon appears deflated, although the volume of helium in the balloon remains constant. When the balloon returns back to room temperature, the molecules inside the balloon move faster, creating a greater force and the balloon resumes its original size and shape. This is an example of how temperature relates to Newton's Third Law that states for every action (the cold temperature), there is an equal and opposite reaction (the warmer temperature).

Motion and Force

AN ACTION REACTION

Purpose

To demonstrate the forces of an equal and opposite reaction.

Curriculum

Newton's Third Law of Motion

Requirements

Time: 5 minutes   *Difficulty Level:* 2

Materials

- 2-liter soda bottle
- rubber stopper or cork that fits the bottle
- cup of vinegar
- baking soda
- 10 round pencils
- funnel
- a flat surface

Safety Note: Do not aim the bottle toward anyone.

Directions

1. On the flat surface, line up the 10 pencils next to each other about 1 inch apart.
2. Place about 1 inch of baking soda in the bottom of the bottle.
3. Use the funnel and fill the bottle with the vinegar.
4. Quickly place the cork on the bottle and lay the bottle sideways on the pencils.
5. Wait for the cork to shoot out of the bottle and observe the movement of the bottle.

Explanation

When the baking soda and vinegar react with each other, carbon dioxide gas is produced. As more gas forms, the pressure in the bottle increases, forcing the stopper to shoot out of the bottle. The shooting stopper is the action force. As this occurs, the bottle rolls backward on the pencils. The movement of the bottle on the pencils is the reaction force. A reaction force is always equal and opposite in direction to an action force. This is an example of Newton's Third Law of Motion.

Variation

Vary the size of the bottle and the amount of vinegar and baking soda.

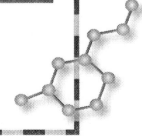

Motion and Force

DUELING BALLOONS

Purpose
To demonstrate what happens when two identical objects share the same air.

Curriculum
Properties of a gas and gas laws; force and motion

Requirements
Time: 2 minutes   *Difficulty Level:* 2

Materials
- two identical balloons (well stretched out)
- two pinch-style clothespins
- empty spool of thread with a single hole through it

Directions
1. Inflate one balloon almost to its maximum fullness.
2. Twist the balloon's neck and clamp it with a clothespin so that no air escapes.
3. Place the open neck of the balloon over one end of the spool.
4. Inflate the second balloon to about ¼ of the size of the first balloon.
5. Clamp it with the second clothespin and place its neck over the other end of the spool.
6. Remove both clothespins at the same time.
7. Observe and discuss.

Explanation
The air flows from the smaller balloon to the bigger balloon because there is more air pressure (or force) in the smaller one. This is the same principle used by utility companies to deliver natural gas to our homes from hundreds, if not thousands, of miles away. After the gas is pumped underground, it is put under high pressure so it can flow along the pipelines. This experiment displays how pressure impacts motion. Low-pressure air always will move toward and into high-pressure air.

Variation
You may try this activity using a 2-inch length of plastic tubing (½-inch diameter) instead of a spool. Also, you may inflate the second balloon to half the size of the first. Then, try the experiment with both balloons inflated to the same size.

Motion and Force

INDY 500

Purpose

To demonstrate the powerful forces of Newton's Motion Laws.

Curriculum

Newton's First and Third Laws of Motion

Requirements

Time: 5 minutes   *Difficulty Level: 2*

Materials

- lightweight, plastic toy car with four movable wheels
- long latex balloon (about 10 inches)
- two-sided adhesive tape
- clean, smooth surface such as a desk

Directions

1. Place the toy car on the smooth surface.
2. Inflate the balloon, pinching the neck of the balloon to keep it inflated. Attach a long piece of tape over the balloon and tape the balloon onto the back of the car, with the opening of the balloon facing the rear of the car.
3. Release the neck of the balloon, allowing it to deflate, and observe the toy car.
4. Discuss.

Explanation

The balloon exerted a force to the car, causing it to move across the table. This force came from air you placed in the balloon that, upon release, pushed the care forward. This is a good example of Newton's First Law of Motion, or inertia. An object (the car) stays at rest or in motion until acted upon by an outside force (the balloon). This activity also demonstrates Newton's Third Law of Motion: For every action, there is an equal and opposite reaction. The air shooting backward pushed the car forward.

Motion and Force

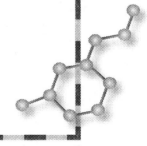

WATER/AIR BALLOON

Purpose
To demonstrate the center of gravity with the forces of air and water.

Curriculum
Center of gravity

Requirements
Time: 2 minutes   *Difficulty Level:* 2

Materials
- one small, round balloon
- one large, round balloon
- water

Directions
1. Fill the small balloon with a small amount of water and tie it.
2. Gently push the water-filled balloon inside the large balloon. This can be difficult, so you may need some help from a friend.
3. Blow up the large balloon and tie it.
4. Play "catch" with the water/air balloon with your friend.
5. Discuss your observations.

Explanation
The water and air balloons wobble as they are thrown because the center of gravity moves around as the balloons fly through the air. The balloon's center of gravity is the water-filled balloon.

Variation
Try different-sized balloons filled with water and air.

Motion and Force

I'M ATTRACTED TO YOU

Purpose

To demonstrate magnetic force.

Curriculum

Magnetic force and water surface tension

Requirements

Time: 2 minutes   *Difficulty Level:* 2

Materials

- 2-quart glass bowl
- sewing needle
- sewing thread
- masking tape
- magnet
- water

Directions

1. Fill the bowl ¾-full with water.
2. Cut two 12-inch pieces of thread.
3. Tape both pieces of thread to one side of the bowl, about 1 inch apart.
4. Stretch the thread across the bowl and lay the needle across both pieces of thread.
5. Slowly lower the thread until the needle rests on the water's surface.
6. Gently move the thread from under the needle. The needle should float on the surface of the water.
7. Move the magnet near, but not touching, the floating needle.
8. Discuss your observations.

Explanation

The needle floats on the surface of the water and moves when the magnet moves. The surface of the water acts like a thin skin that we call surface tension. The needle moves across the surface of the water in response to the magnetic force of attraction exuded by the magnet.

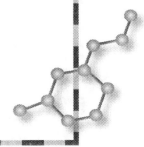

JET ENGINE BALLOON

Purpose

To illustrate the principles of jet propulsion.

Curriculum

Air pressure and Newton's Third Law of Motion

Requirements

Time: 5 minutes   *Difficulty Level:* 3

Materials

- 10 feet of thick thread or string
- long balloon (about 10 inches)
- plastic drinking straw
- tape
- two sturdy chairs or movable pieces of furniture

Directions

1. Push one end of the string though the straw.
2. Tie one end of the string to one of the chairs.
3. Stretch the string across the room and tie it the other chair.
4. Pull on the second chair and make the string very taut, but do not pull on the string so hard that you break it.
5. Blow up the balloon and hold the end so the air doesn't escape.
6. Tape the balloon onto the straw with two pieces of tape, using one strip of tape in front and one in back. Make sure that the balloon doesn't deflate.
7. Move the balloon-straw combination back to the end of the chair. Make sure the end of the balloon you are holding is pointed away from the long end of the string.
8. Release the balloon and observe.

Explanation

When you let go of the balloon, the air pushes the balloon forward. Change in pressure is what enables a jet engine to propel an airplane. This is the same action and reaction that moved the balloon down the string. This activity demonstrates Newton's Third Law of Motion: When an object exerts a force upon another, the second object exerts an equal and opposite force upon the first object. The action in a jet engine is the exhaust from the engine; the reaction is the jet engine moving forward. Jets need oxygen to burn fuel, which gives the engine energy. In the case of this balloon experiment, the energy came from your breath.

Motion and Force

WACKY SPACE SHUTTLE

Procedure

To show how pressure increases when gas is produced.

Curriculum

Air pressure and gas formation

Requirements

Time: 5 minutes   *Difficulty Level:* 3

Materials

- clear, plastic 2-liter soda bottle
- cork or rubber stopper that will fit in the mouth of the 2-liter bottle
- ½ cup of vinegar
- 2 tablespoons of baking soda
- piece of toilet paper or facial tissue

Directions

1. Pour the vinegar in the soda bottle.
2. Place the baking soda on a piece of facial tissue. Wrap the baking soda in the tissue tight enough so that this bundle will fit tight through the neck of the bottle.
3. Tilt the bottle at a slight angle and drop the tissue paper into it.
4. Place the cork firmly (but not too tightly) into the neck of the bottle, and allow the paper to drop into the vinegar. Stand the bottle erect or place it at a slight angle, aimed away from yourself and any observers. Wait for the launch.
5. Discuss your observations.

Safety Note: This activity should be a teacher demonstration or, at least, adult-monitored. Perform this activity outdoors.

Explanation

As the liquid slowly soaks through the paper, the reaction of the baking soda and vinegar produces carbon dioxide gas. As more gas forms, pressure increases in the closed container until it is great enough to force the cork out of the bottle. Like with any object, including polymers, there is a breaking point when too much pressure is applied.

Variation

Attach a few streamers or pieces of ribbon to the cork for a colorful effect.

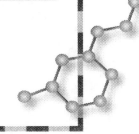

Motion and Force

BUTTON YOUR FLY-WHEEL

Procedure

To illustrate the principles of inertia and motion.

Curriculum

Newton's First Law of Motion

Requirements

Time: 5 minutes   *Difficulty Level:* 4

Materials

- 2 feet of string
- buttons with multiple holes

Directions

1. Thread about 2 feet of string through one hole in the button and back through an opposite hole.
2. Tie the string ends together.
3. Center the button in the middle.
4. Hold each end of the string, one end in each hand, and twirl the button until the string and button are tightly wound. (The double strands of the string will be twisted around each other.)
5. Start pulling on the string quickly and the button will spin very rapidly.
6. After the string has untwisted, if you hold it loose and do not move it, the button will keep on moving and will wind up again. (However it will go in the opposite direction.)
7. Discuss your observations.

Explanation

What you made is called a flywheel. Flywheels abide by the principle that objects at rest tend to remain at rest and objects in motion tend to keep moving in a straight line (Newton's First Law of Motion). It takes little energy to keep your flywheel moving at a high speed.

Variation

Try various-sized buttons and strings for making different flywheels.

Motion and Force

The Pressure Is On

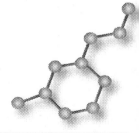

Almost everyone is familiar with the word pressure—but perhaps the first thing that comes to students' minds is the pressure they feel to get good grades. In this section, you and your students will look at pressure from a scientific perspective. The activities in this section are focused on air and water pressure, which can be measured and observed. If you teach younger students, they may not think of air and water having pressure, but after this section, you will have them convinced. The pressure is on!

BUT IT WON'T FILL UP 46

FLY AWAY. 47

HUFF 'N' PUFF. 48

WITHOUT SPILLING A DROP. 49

DING, DONG DIVER. 50

WATERWORKS 51

GENIE IN THE BOTTLE. 52

THE CLEAN MACHINE. 53

BLAST OFF 54

BOTTLE FOUNTAIN 55

NO JOKING MATTER. 56

WATER, WATER EVERYWHERE, BUT NOT A DROP TO DRINK 57

BUT IT WON'T FILL UP

Purpose

To demonstrate how lack of pressure affects gravity.

Curriculum

Air pressure

Requirements

Time: 2 minutes   *Difficulty Level:* 1

Materials

- funnel
- empty soda bottle
- small piece of clay
- water

Directions

1. Place the funnel in the neck of the empty soda bottle.
2. Place clay around the neck of the bottle so that there is no air around or between the funnel and the bottle.
3. Pour water in the funnel and observe.
4. Remove the clay and observe.

Explanation

While the clay is on the neck of the bottle, the water remains in the funnel or enters in slow spurts. When the bottle is sealed, the volume of water entering the bottle pushes out an equal volume of oxygen from the bottle. The clay forms a seal around the bottle's mouth, forcing the escaping air to bubble through the mouth of the bottle (where the funnel is). The transfer of air for water inside the bottle will happen at a very slow rate. This seems to defy gravity, but it is simply matter of an air-pressure situation. When the clay is removed and the air is able to leave around the neck of the bottle, the water can flow into the bottle. This proves that air takes up space and has pressure.

FLY AWAY

Purpose

To illustrate the movement of air due to unequal pressure.

Curriculum

Air pressure

Requirements

Time: 1 minute   *Difficulty Level:* 1

Materials

- empty, narrow-necked soda bottle
- small piece of paper (about 1 inch x 1 inch)

Directions

1. Lay the soda bottle on its side.
2. Crumple the paper into a small wad and place it just inside the mouth of the bottle. The wad should fit loosely.
3. Try to blow the paper wad into the bottle with your breath.

Explanation

Before you blow into the bottle, the amount of air inside and outside the bottle is the same. The extra air blown into the bottle increases the air pressure inside. This extra air is pushed out of the opening, and the moving air swishes the paper wad out of the bottle.

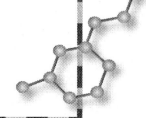

HUFF 'N' PUFF

Purpose

To demonstrate that air takes up space.

Curriculum

Air and matter

Requirements

Time: 1 minute   *Difficulty Level:* 1

Materials

- balloon
- empty glass soda bottle

Directions

1. Push the deflated balloon into the bottle and stretch the open end back over the bottle's mouth.
2. Blow into the balloon as hard as you can.

Explanation

As you inflate the balloon, it takes up additional space in the bottle. But, the bottle is already full of air before you begin. Even though you cannot see it, this air takes up space. When you try to blow up the balloon, the air trapped inside the bottle prevents you from doing it.

WITHOUT SPILLING A DROP

Purpose

To illustrate the difference between surface tension and air pressure.

Curriculum

Surface area and water pressure

Requirements

Time: 1 minute   *Difficulty Level:* 1

Materials

- 8-ounce drinking glass
- playing card large enough to cover the mouth of the glass
- water

Directions

1. Fill the glass to the top with water.
2. Place the card on top of the glass.
3. While holding the card, quickly invert the glass.
4. Remove your hand from the card. The water and card should remain in place, at least temporarily.

Explanation

Surface tension between the glass and water, and between the water and card, hold the water in place. Air pressure also helps this work. When the glass is inverted, a few drops of water leak out. This increases the volume of air inside the glass and decreases the air pressure inside the glass. The airs pressure outside pushes the card against the mouth, holding it on the water.

Variation

Fill the glass with different amounts of water and observe what happens. Try a different shape or size of glass and use different types of coverings.

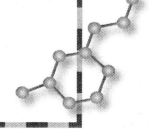

DING, DONG DIVER

Purpose

To illustrate the nature of fluid pressure.

Curriculum

Fluid pressure and a Cartesian Diver

Requirements

Time: 1 minute   *Difficulty Level:* 2

Materials

- 1-liter or smaller plastic soda bottle
- eyedropper
- water

Directions

1. Fill the bottle to the very top with water.
2. Fill the eyedropper about half full of water.
3. Place the dropper in the soda bottle. The dropper should be standing upright in the bottle. (If not, take the eyedropper out, add more water, and replace the eyedropper.) Cap the bottle.
4. Squeeze the bottle firmly with both hands and observe the result.

Explanation

When you squeezed the bottle, the dropper fell down to the bottom of the bottle because you forced water into the eyedropper, increasing its mass. When you released the bottle, the dropper returned to its original position (standing upright) because you decreased the water pressure from the dropper. The water was expelled from the dropper and was replaced with air. Thus, the mass became less and the dropper rose accordingly. This activity is often called the "Cartesian Diver" and is a classic science experiment.

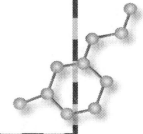

WATERWORKS

Purpose

To demonstrate how heat affects water pressure.

Curriculum

Temperature changes and water pressure

Requirements

Time: 5 minutes   *Difficulty Level:* 2

Materials

- plastic turkey baster
- stove or other heating source
- small pan
- water
- oven mitt or protective glove

Directions

1. Suck up some of the cold water with the baster, and quickly turn the baster over. Observe. Then empty the baster.
2. Heat a small pan with water until the water is near the boiling point.
3. Wearing an oven mitt, suck up some of the hot water with the baster and quickly turn the baster over. (Do not squeeze the bulb of the baster.)
4. Observe and discuss.

Explanation

When you turned over the baster of cold water, nothing happened. However, you observed the hot water shoot out of the turkey baster. This happened because when you heated the water, you also increased the water pressure. Warm air and water particles move faster than cold air and water particles; therefore, they exert a higher pressure. This pressure was strong enough to push the water out of the baster without having to squeeze the bulb.

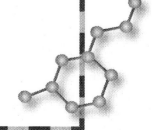

GENIE IN THE BOTTLE

Purpose

To exhibit the change in air volume caused by temperature change.

Curriculum

Vacuum formation and air pressure

Requirements

Time: 5 minutes   *Difficulty Level:* 3

Materials

- 2- or 3-liter plastic soda bottle (label removed)
- hot plate, stove, or other heat source
- pot
- oven mitt
- funnel
- bowl full of ice and cold water

Directions

1. Boil about 1 cup of water in the pot.
2. Using the funnel, carefully pour the hot water into the plastic bottle.
3. Wearing the mitt, turn the bottle back and forth so the water swishes around in the bottle for a couple of minutes, heating up the air in the bottle.
4. Empty the hot water from the bottle and immediately invert the bottle over the bowl of ice-cold water, keeping the neck of the bottle slightly under the surface of the water at all times.
5. Hold the bottle in place for a minute or so and observe the water rise several inches into the plastic bottle.

Safety Note: Use caution when pouring the hot water into the bottle. Avoid spilling the water out of the bottle in Step 3.

Explanation

When the heated air in the bottle cooled, a vacuum was formed, because cool air takes up less space than hot air. The water was pushed into the bottle by the pressure of the surrounding air.

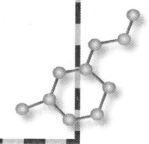

THE CLEAN MACHINE

Purpose

To explain how water goes through a filtration process.

Curriculum

Waste-water treatment

Requirements

Time: 15 minutes   *Difficulty Level:* 3

Materials

- clean, 1-quart clay flower pot with a hole at the bottom
- two coffee filters
- pie pan
- 1 cup each of crushed charcoal, sand, and gravel
- water from a nearby lake, pond, or river
- two glass jars

Directions

1. Line the clay pot with the two coffee filters and set the pot in the pie pan.
2. Place a cup of each material in the filter in this order: charcoal, sand, and gravel, with the charcoal on the bottom.
3. Fill both glass jars with your water sample and observe. Notice the water's color or any foreign matter in the water.
4. Pour the water from one of the jars into the clay pot filter and allow it to filter all the way through. This may take 5 to 10 minutes, depending on the size of your filtering materials and quality of your water.
5. Once the water is filtered, pour it from the pie pan back into the original jar.
6. Now compare the two samples.

Explanation

Notice how much cleaner the filtered water is. This is a simple model of how a water-treatment filtration plants work. The large particles are trapped on top while the smaller particles are trapped near the bottom. Chemicals are added before and after the treatment process to kill many types of germs and bacteria.

Variation

Try different types of filtering materials in different quantities. Consider a visit to your local waste-water treatment facility.

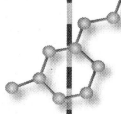

BLAST OFF

Purpose

To illustrate the principle of rocket engines.

Curriculum

Jet propulsion

Requirements

Time: 5 minutes   *Difficulty Level:* 4

Materials

- 2-liter clear plastic soda bottle
- rubber stopper (must fit halfway into the soda bottle)
- inflating needle
- bicycle tire air pump
- ice pick
- water

Directions

1. Place 1 cup of water into the bottle.
2. Using the ice pick, carefully make a hole in the center of the rubber stopper to allow the needle to be inserted.
3. Attach the needle to the pump.
4. Place the stopper snugly into the bottle. Do not force it in.
5. Place the bottle on its side. Aim the bottle into the open area and begin to pump air into the bottle. Do not pause as you pump, as the water will back up into the pump.
6. Discuss your observations as a class.

Safety Note: Teacher activity only, or adult supervision required. Do this activity outdoors only. Caution any observers to stand at a safe distance.

Explanation

As air is pumped into the bottle, the pressure inside the bottle will increase. As the pressure continues to increase inside the bottle, the stopper was pushed out, which caused the air and water inside the bottle to rush out, thus creating a rocket engine effect. Your bottle will launch with a powerful "whoosh!"

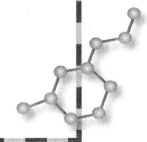

BOTTLE FOUNTAIN

Purpose

To demonstrate how temperature change affects water pressure.

Curriculum

Water pressure and temperature change

Requirements

Time: 10 minutes   *Difficulty Level:* 4

Materials

- 12- or 16-ounce plastic soda bottle with screw-top cap
- nail or sharp instrument
- silicone sealant, caulk, or similar sealer
- very hot water (from a running tap)
- ice cold water
- large bowl
- clear drinking straw

Directions

1. Carefully cut a hole with the nail in the top of the screw cap that is big enough for the straw to pass through.
2. Screw the cap on the bottle.
3. Push the straw through the hole about halfway.
4. Seal up the gap between the screw cap and the straw with the sealant. This seal has to be airtight. You may have to allow the sealant to dry before you proceed, depending on the type of sealant used.
5. Carefully remove the cap and fill the bottle with the ice cold water.
6. Screw the cap on the bottle very tightly.
7. Fill the bowl with very hot water.
8. Place the bottle in the hot water.
9. Discuss your observations as a class.

Safety Note: Use caution when piercing the bottle cap.

Explanation

The water will shoot out of the straw like a park fountain because when the cold water was placed in the bottle, it cooled the surrounding air molecules. The hot water then heated up those molecules and caused the air to expand. The expanding air pressed down on the water and forced it up the straw.

NO JOKING MATTER

Purpose

To demonstrate how an emulsion can be used to copy print from a newspaper.

Curriculum

Mixtures and solutions

Requirements

Time: 5 minutes   *Difficulty Level:* 4

Materials

- 2 tablespoons of turpentine
- 2 tablespoons of liquid detergent
- 4 tablespoons of water
- small mixing bowl or cup
- small piece of sponge
- comic strip or cartoons from a newspaper (color or black and white)
- blank piece of writing paper
- spoon

Directions

1. Mix the water, turpentine, and liquid detergent in the bowl.
2. Dab the liquid with the sponge, then onto the comic strip or cartoon you wish to copy.
3. Lay the writing paper on top of the comic.
4. Rub vigorously with the spoon until the image is clearly transferred to the writing paper.
5. Hold the cartoon up to a mirror.

Safety Note: Use caution with turpentine; it is a flammable substance.

Explanation

You will have made a mirror copy of the cartoon, that is, the image will be printed backwards. Turpentine and liquid detergent form an emulsion capable of penetrating between the dye and oil particles of the dry printing ink, making the newsprint ink liquid again. Newspaper print ink dissolves easily; however, glossy magazine paper contains too much lacquer and is not suitable for this activity.

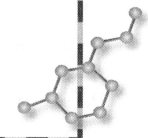

WATER, WATER EVERYWHERE, BUT NOT A DROP TO DRINK

Purpose

To display an unusual way to display air and water pressure.

Curriculum

Water and air pressure

Requirements

Time: 5 minutes (plus painting and drying *Time*)   *Difficulty Level:* 4

Materials

- 2-liter plastic soda bottle
- water
- brush
- one foot of ⅞-inch (outside diameter) vinyl tubing
- scissors
- small nail or punch
- any color paint
- container (to catch the water)

Directions

1. Place the vinyl tubing in the opening of the bottle, leaving it about ½ inch from the bottom. (The fit will be very tight, but this is what you want.)
2. Cut off any excess tubing level with the top of the bottle with scissors.
3. Paint the soda bottle so you cannot see the contents inside.
4. Using the nail, punch a small hole at the top of the bottle to the side of the cap.
5. Fill the bottle with water.
6. Occasionally pour water out of the bottle into the empty container, but make sure you hold your finger over the pinhole whenever you pour it.
7. Now, uncover the hole and observe that water will be forced up the tube when the bottle is set upright.

Safety Note: Use caution when punching a hole in the bottle.

Explanation

When the bottle is filled with water and the hole left at the top of the bottle is left open, air pressure will force water up the tube. If the hole is covered and the bottle is inverted, only the water in the tube will come out. Set the bottle upright, with the hole left open and the tube will refill. The purpose of painting the bottle is to allow observers to use their imagination as to what is happening in the bottle during the experiment.

Variation

Suggest that students make a drawing of what they hypothesize happens during this activity.

Hot and Cold Stuff

Describe this scenario to students: You pick up two friends from the airport at the same time. One flew in from the North Pole, the other from a country along the Equator. The friend from the North Pole says that she thinks it is very warm today, whereas the friend from the Equator says he thinks that it very cold. Why is this? They are both experiencing the same weather conditions. Explain to students that hot and cold are relative terms and don't mean much without a frame of reference, which in this case is where you live. Most people live in climates that have variations in temperature, ranging from hot to cold. For many of us, the seasons bring distinct changes: temperatures will vary from hot or mild, to cold and then back to hot again.

Temperature is a significant factor in everyday life. Your students might check the thermometer or weather reports to decide how to dress for the day. In this section, you and your students will take a look at hot and cold from a different perspective.

COOL IT 60

FOLLOW THE BOUNCING BALL 61

SWEATY PALMS 62

JUST HOW BIG IS WATER, ANYWAY? 63

MOTHBALL FROST 64

PLOP, PLOP, FIZZ, FIZZ 65

A CUT ABOVE 66

COLLAPSING BOTTLE 67

POLAR BEAR IN UNDERWEAR 68

THE ICEBERG 69

DEW PROCESS 70

HI, SWEETIE PIE! 71

PRESERVING SNOWFLAKES 72

COOL IT

Purpose

To illustrate how evaporation affects the cooling process.

Curriculum

Phase change

Requirements

Time: 1 minute   *Difficulty Level:* 1

Materials

- small amount of rubbing alcohol
- two cotton balls
- water
- the back side of both hands

Directions

1. With the cotton ball, dab the back of one hand with the rubbing alcohol.
2. With the other cotton ball, dab the back of your other hand with some water.
3. At the same time, wave both hands in the air and note which hand feels colder.

Safety Note: Do not get the alcohol in an open cut; it will burn.

Explanation

Heat is absorbed from the surface of your skin as the water and alcohol evaporates. Therefore, the temperature of your body is lowered. Alcohol evaporates faster than water. The more rapid evaporation of alcohol results in greater coolness. This is why you feel cooler when you step out of the shower or you rub on alcohol if you have a high fever.

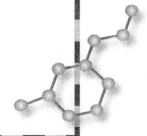

FOLLOW
THE BOUNCING BALL

Purpose

To determine how temperature affects the bounce of a ball.

Curriculum

Temperature and molecular movement

Requirements

Time: 1 minute plus 30 minutes freezing time   *Difficulty Level:* 1

Materials

- tennis ball
- yardstick
- refrigerator with a freezer

Directions

1. Hold the yardstick with one hand and place the ball at the top of its edge.
2. Release the ball and measure the height of its bounce. (Optional: Repeat this step three times, and get the average reading.)
3. Place the ball in the freezer for 30 minutes.
4. Repeat Steps 1 and 2.

Explanation

The ball does not bounce as high after it is placed in the freezer because the molecules are moving more slowly due to the cold. The warmer the materials, the faster the molecules will move. The faster the molecules move, the higher the bounce of the ball. Playing tennis in cold weather would have an effect on your game.

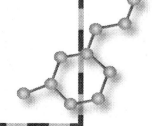

SWEATY PALMS

Purpose

To show how liquids pass through skin pores.

Curriculum

Human physiology

Requirements

Time: 15 minutes   *Difficulty Level:* 1

Materials

- clear plastic bag large enough to cover your hand
- string
- dry hand
- a partner

Directions

1. Place your hand in the plastic bag.
2. Have your partner tie a piece of string around your wrist to hold the bag in place.
3. Keep the bag on your hand for about 15 minutes and observe.

Explanation

Small droplets of water began forming on the inside of the bag. The moisture is from the pores of your skin. Your hand was actually sweating, and the moisture was not able to evaporate because the bag trapped the sweat. Sweating gets rid of extra water from your body, which is why your body sweats on hot days.

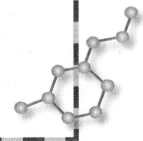

JUST HOW BIG IS WATER, ANYWAY?

Purpose

To demonstrate the expansion and contraction of water.

Curriculum

Kinetic theory

Requirements

Time: 5 minutes (plus several hours of cooling and freezing time) *Difficulty Level:* 2

Materials

- water
- stove or other heat source
- dry erase marker
- small pan
- three glass baby food jars
- refrigerator with a freezer
- piece of cardboard

Directions

Part A:

1. Fill one baby food jar to the brim with water and place it in a pan.
2. Fill the pan with several inches of water.
3. Heat the jar in the pan on medium heat. Do not boil.
4. Observe the level of the water.

Part B:

1. Fill the second baby food jar half full with water. Draw a line with the dry erase marker to mark the height of the water in the jar.
2. Place the jar in a refrigerator for several hours.
3. Observe the level of the water.

Part C:

1. Fill the third baby food jar to the brim with water.
2. Set the jar on a flat surface in the freezer and place the cardboard on top of the jar.
3. After several hours (or until the water is frozen) observe the level of the water and the cardboard.

Explanation

A. Water, like other liquids, fills more space when heated. The molecules bounce against one another more rapidly and spread out.

B. Until the temperature of water drops to 39 degrees Fahrenheit, water contracts (takes up less space) as it gets colder. The molecules move more slowly and get closer together.

C. When the temperature of water goes below 39 degrees to its freezing point of 32 degrees, it expands. It is one of the few liquids to behave this way.

MOTHBALL FROST

Purpose
To display how matter can change from a solid to a vapor then return to a solid.

Curriculum
Sublimation and crystallization

Requirements
Time: 10 minutes   *Difficulty Level:* 2

Materials
- a mothball or moth flakes
- jar with a lid
- pan
- water
- stove or other heating source

Directions
1. Place one mothball in the jar and place the lid on the jar.
2. Fill the pan with water and place it on the stove.
3. Place the jar in the pan and heat gently until the mothball changes to a vapor.
4. Remove the jar from the heat and allow cooling. Observe.

Safety Note: Avoid touching the mothball and do not inhale the vapors that the mothball gives off.

Explanation
Mothballs change directly from a solid to an invisible vapor. The mothball gets smaller and smaller until it eventually disappears. This process is called sublimation. This vapor is what actually repels moths. When the vapor is removed from the heat, it cools and changes back to a solid in the forms of crystals. Crystals start growing by a process called "nucleation." Nucleation can begin growing with the molecules themselves, or with the help of some solid matter already in the solution.

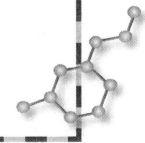

Hot and Cold Stuff

PLOP, PLOP, FIZZ, FIZZ

Purpose
To exhibit how a reaction rate can be affected by temperature.

Curriculum
Reaction rates

Requirements
Time: 10 minutes   *Difficulty Level:* 2

Materials
- three baby food jars
- three Alka-Seltzer tablets
- cold water
- hot water
- room temperature tap water
- clock with a second hand

Hot and Cold Stuff

Directions
1. Pour cold water in one jar, room temperature water in another jar, and hot water into the third jar.
2. Drop one Alka-Seltzer tablet, at the same time, into each one of the jars.
3. Time how long it takes for each tablet to completely dissolve.
4. Discuss the time differences.

Explanation
Molecules move faster when the temperature is warmer. The warmer the liquid, the faster the molecules move; therefore, the faster the rate of reaction (and dissolving). The opposite also is true, the colder the liquid, the slower the molecules move and the slower the reaction rate.

Variation
Use different liquids and graph your results.

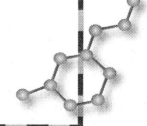

A CUT ABOVE

Purpose
To illustrate how heat can be intensified.

Curriculum
Solar energy and optics

Requirements
Time: **5 minutes**   *Difficulty Level:* 3

Materials
- piece of string (not thread)
- tape
- 1-quart clear glass jar with a lid
- magnifying glass

Directions
1. Tape the top of the string to the middle of the inside of the jar lid.
2. Insert the string into the jar and screw on the lid.
3. With the string hanging in the jar, go outdoors or near a window on a sunny day.
4. With the magnifying glass, focus the rays of the sun on the string for a few minutes. Hold the magnifier steady at any one specific spot on the string.
5. Observe and discuss the results.

Explanation
The string should break as the magnifying glass concentrates the heat of the sun on one spot of the string. The heat will become intense enough to burn right through the string because you are increasing the concentration of the sun's energy to one location.

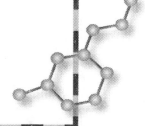

Hot and Cold Stuff

COLLAPSING BOTTLE

Purpose

To illustrate how warm air takes up more space than cold air.

Curriculum

Vacuum formation

Requirements

Time: **5 minutes**   *Difficulty Level:* 3

Materials

- empty 2-liter plastic soda bottle with cap
- stove or other heating source
- pan
- funnel
- water
- sink

Directions

1. Heat a pan of water on the stove until it is nearly boiling.
2. Using the funnel, fill the soda bottle about ¼ of the way with the hot water.
3. Tightly screw the cap on the bottle.
4. Gently shake the bottle for 30 seconds.
5. Remove the cap and immediately empty the bottle in the sink.
6. Quickly screw the cap back on.
7. Set the bottle down and observe.

Explanation

The bottle collapsed. Warm air takes up more space because its molecules move faster than cold air particles. As the air inside the bottle cools down, the air takes up less space so that the air pressure outside the bottle is greater than air pressure inside the bottle. This causes a partial vacuum on the inside, and the bottle implodes.

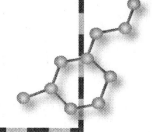

POLAR BEAR IN UNDERWEAR

Purpose
To illustrate how fat acts as an insulator against cold.

Curriculum
Temperature and insulators

Requirements
Time: 5 minutes   *Difficulty Level:* 3

Materials
- 2-quart sized Ziploc® bags
- solid vegetable shortening (such as Crisco)
- spoon
- tub of cold water

Directions
1. Turn a baggie inside out and spread a ½-inch thick layer of the shortening on the inside of the first bag. Try not to get any of the shortening on the zip closure area.
2. Carefully slip the second bag over the bag of shortening so that the shortening layer is between the two bags.
3. On the non-shortening side, spread another layer of shortening between the two bags.
4. Zip-lock the two bags together.
5. Place one hand in the "glove's" opening.
6. Place both hands in the tub of ice water.

Explanation
When both hands are placed in the water, the hand with the glove feels very warm because the protective layer of fat acts as an insulator. The solid shortening is pure fat, and fat is what protects polar bears in cold climates from the frigid climate and icy arctic waters.

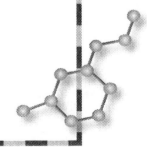

THE ICEBERG

Purpose

To illustrate the carving effect of an iceberg.

Curriculum

Density and earth's changes

Requirements

Time: 5 minutes (plus overnight freezing time) *Difficulty Level:* 3

Materials

- 6–8-inch balloon
- cup of sand and/or fine gravel mixture
- freezer
- funnel
- plastic bag (large enough to fit in the filled balloon)
- scissors
- deep bucket
- water

Directions

1. Fit the balloon over a cold water faucet and fill it about ¾ full of water.
2. Place the funnel in the mouth of the balloon and add the sand and gravel mixture.
3. Tie the end of the balloon.
4. Place the filled balloon in the plastic bag and leave it in the freezer overnight.
5. Remove the balloon from the bag and carefully cut away the balloon material from the frozen water. You now have an iceberg.
6. Put your iceberg in a deep bucket that is filled with water and observe.

Explanation

You will notice only a small amount of the ice is exposed over the surface of the water. The weight of the sand and gravel is greater than the ice; therefore, it sinks below the water level. Because the entire iceberg is less dense than the surrounding water, it will float.

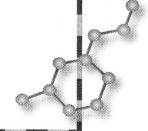

DEW PROCESS

Purpose

To demonstrate how fog and dew are created.

Curriculum

Weather

Requirements

Time: 15 minutes   *Difficulty Level:* 4

Materials

- glass jar with a narrow mouth
- cup of hot water
- pan (to heat the water)
- heat source
- ice cubes
- small plastic sandwich bag
- metal can

Directions

Part A:
1. Heat the water on a heat source and pour the hot water into the glass jar.
2. Place the ice cubes in the bag and put the bag over the mouth of the jar. Do not allow the ice cubes to fall in the water.
3. In a few minutes, notice what happens inside the jar.

Part B:
1. Place a handful of ice cubes inside a perfectly dry metal can.
2. Wait a few minutes; notice what happens on the outside of the can.

Note: This activity works best when the relative humidity in the room is over 50%.

Explanation

A. The hot water makes the air in the jar warm and moist. The warm, moist air rises toward the top of the jar where it is suddenly cooled by the ice. As the temperature drops, the water condenses into small drops, making a swirling fog inside the jar.

B. The temperature of the air outside the can is lowered when it comes in contact with the ice-filled can. The water vapor in the air condenses (from a gas to a liquid) on the side of the can, forming dew. The temperature at which dew first appears is called the dew-point.

Hot and Cold Stuff

HI, SWEETIE PIE!

Purpose

To demonstrate the conditions that affect the dissolving rate of a substance.

Curriculum

Hot and cold temperature; molecular movement

Requirements

Time: 10 minutes   *Difficulty Level:* 4

Materials

- four sugar cubes
- two plastic spoons
- a dry-erase marker
- stove or other heating source
- ice cubes
- two sheets of paper
- four jars (of the same size)
- two plastic sandwich bags
- pan
- water

Directions

1. Wrap two sugar cubes separately in a piece of paper.
2. Place each cube in a separate plastic bag and crush the cubes into powder by stepping on the bags.
3. With the marker, label two jars "hot" and two jars "cold."
4. Fill the two "hot" jars half full with hot water.
5. Fill the two "cold" jars with cold water and add several ice cubes to each "cold" jar.
6. Pour a crushed sugar cube into one of the "hot" jars, and drop a whole sugar cube into the other "hot" jar.
7. Stir each container with your spoon and count to measure the amount of time it takes for the sugar to dissolve.
8. Repeat Steps 6 and 7 with the cold jars of water.
9. Discuss any differences that you observed.

Explanation

You should have noticed that the hot water dissolved the crushed sugar much faster than the cold water dissolved the whole cube. Coming in second place should either be cold water/crushed cube or the hot water/whole cube. The smaller the particles of a solute (sugar cube), the faster the solute will disappear (dissolve). The warmer the temperature of the solvent (water), the faster the solute will dissolve. In other words, when you increase temperature and surface area, you increase the rate of reaction.

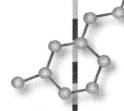

PRESERVING SNOWFLAKES

Purpose

To collect and preserve snowflake samples for a closer analysis.

Curriculum

Crystallization

Requirements

Snowy weather conditions
Time: 5 minutes (plus one hour chill time and one hour dry time)
Difficulty Level: 4

Materials

- a microscope slide or a thin, small piece of glass
- clear lacquer spray
- clothes pin
- hand lens or magnifying glass

Directions

1. Chill the glass slide outdoors in a protected area for 1 hour.
2. When it starts to snow, attach the clothespin to one end of the slide.
3. Hold the slide by the clothespin so your body heat won't warm the slide.
4. Spray the slide with a thin coat of lacquer. (You may want to slightly chill the lacquer so it also will not warm up the slide.)
5. Catch a few snowflakes on your slide.
6. Leave the slide outside in the cold, but in a protected place where the snow will not fall on it.
7. Bring your slide inside and examine the snowflakes' imprints in the lacquer using the hand lens or magnifying glass.
8. Discuss the characteristics of the snowflakes.

Explanation

The snowflake imprints remains permanent in the non-water-soluble lacquer after the snowflakes melt and the slide dries. Water has interesting thermal properties. When heated from 0°C, its melting point, to 4°C, it contracts and becomes more dense; most other substances expand and become less dense when heated. Conversely, when water is cooled in this temperature range, it expands. It expands greatly as it freezes; as a consequence, ice is less dense than water and floats on it.

Hot and Cold Stuff

In Living Color

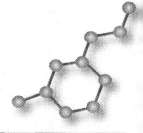

Read this scenario to students: One morning as you dress for school, you notice that your new red jacket does not look the same as it did in the store when you bought it. At school your friends compliment you as they see it. You look at your jacket and notice again that the color looks different from the way it did at home! What's going on, you ask yourself? Shouldn't everything look the same when you see it in the light? In this section, you and your students will take a new look at colors and see how they relate to the world around you.

GREEN-GOBBULLY-GUKK 74

RAINBOW BRIGHT 75

FANCY COLORS 76

I'M SEEING RED NOW 77

COLOR CREATIONS 78

WHAT COLOR IS BLACK? 79

SOMEWHERE OVER THE RAINBOW 80

SPINSATIONAL COLOR DISK 81

THE CRYSTAL GARDEN 82

WE EAT AND DRINK ACIDS AND BASES 83

GREEN-GOBBULLY-GUKK

Purpose

To demonstrate the chemical properties of a metal.

Curriculum

Chemistry and chemical reactions

Requirements

Time: 1 minute (plus 24-hour setup)   *Difficulty Level:* 1

Materials

- 4 pennies
- paper towel
- vinegar
- bowl

Directions

1. Fold the paper towel in quarters.
2. Place the folded towel in the bowl.
3. Place enough vinegar into the bowl to wet the towel thoroughly.
4. Place the pennies on top of the wet towel.
5. Wait 24 hours and then observe and discuss any changes.

Explanation

After 24 hours have elapsed, the tops of the pennies have turned green. The acetate part of the acid combines with the copper on the pennies to form the green coating, a compound called copper acetate. Color change is one of several indicators that a chemical change has taken place.

In Living Color

RAINBOW BRIGHT

Purpose
To demonstrate the presence of colors in sunlight.

Curriculum
Temperature and molecular movement

Requirements
Time: 2 minutes   *Difficulty Level:* 1

Materials
- clear bowl
- water
- small hand mirror
- sunlight

Directions
1. Fill the clear bowl with water.
2. Set the bowl next to a window in direct sunlight.
3. Place the hand mirror in the water.
4. Angle the mirror until the sun is reflected and the spectrum of colors shine on a nearby object.

Explanation
Light is made up of many colors, and when light passes at an angle from air to water (both being transparent), the light separates into a color spectrum. Sometimes after a rainstorm, there is still a lot of water in the air and a rainbow will form as the sun comes out and shines through the mist.

In Living Color

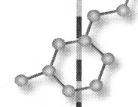

FANCY COLORS

Purpose
To demonstrate how colors are affected by differences in density.

Curriculum
Density and color

Requirements
Time: 10 minutes   *Difficulty Level:* 2

Materials
- clear glass bowl
- 1 tablespoon of cooking oil
- food coloring (red, blue, and green)
- fork
- water
- cup

Directions
1. Fill the bowl ¾ full of water.
2. Pour 1 tablespoon of cooking oil into the cup and add four drops of each color of food coloring.
3. Use the fork to beat the oil and food coloring thoroughly.
4. Pour the oil-and-food-coloring mixture into a bowl of water.
5. Observe the action on the surface of the water.

Explanation
The colors appear to explode outward, producing circles of color on the water with color streams that sink downward. Oil and water are different densities and do not mix well. Food coloring is water-based, so it is isolated in tiny spheres though the oil. The colored spheres sink through the oil layer and dissolve in the water below.

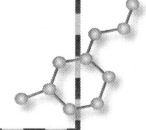

I'M SEEING RED NOW

Purpose

To demonstrate a chemical reaction between an acid and base.

Curriculum

Acid and base reaction

Requirements

Time: 5 minutes   *Difficulty Level:* 2

Materials

- spray bottle of ammonia glass cleaner
- turmeric spice seasoning
- rubbing alcohol
- paper towel
- small brush
- cup
- spoon

Directions

1. In the cup, place 1 tablespoon of turmeric seasoning (in its dry powder form) and 4 ounces of rubbing alcohol. Stir thoroughly.
2. Dipping a brush in this mixture, print a message on the paper towel. Allow your message to dry for a couple of seconds.
3. Hold the towel in one hand and the spray bottle in the other hand. Gently spray the towel until you can read your message.

Safety Note: Use caution when spraying the window cleaner. Turmeric will stain clothing. Do this activity outdoors or over a container to catch the dripping liquid. Avoid inhaling fumes.

Explanation

Turmeric is a mild chemical acid. As a finely ground powder, the turmeric dissolves in the alcohol. The glass cleaner contains ammonia, which is a chemical base. As this base hits the acid that has been applied to the paper towel, the vivid red color appears. The root of the turmeric plant has been used for hundreds of years for dyeing ,as well as for seasoning food. It also is used in chemistry to make test papers for bases (alkalis), a purpose that this experiment demonstrates.

In Living Color

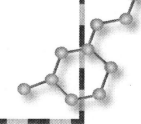

COLOR CREATIONS

Purpose
To show how colors are created.

Curriculum
Primary and complementary colors

Requirements
Time: 5 minutes   *Difficulty Level:* 3

Materials
- three empty baby food jars
- water
- food coloring (red, yellow, and blue)
- three medicine droppers
- Styrofoam egg cartons
- paper towels (for spills)
- gallon-size plastic container

Directions
1. Fill the baby food jars ⅔ full of water.
2. Add several drops of red food coloring to the first baby food jar. Add several drops of yellow to the second jar, and several drops of blue to the third jar. Stir.
3. Using a different eyedropper for each color, fill one dropper with each color of water and squeeze each into a separate section of the egg carton.
4. Mix and match the different colors by combining them in the egg carton sections until they are all full.
5. Observe and discuss the color combinations.
6. Experiment even more by dumping all of the colors into your empty plastic container.

Explanation
You can create many different color combinations by using the three primary colors of red, blue, and yellow. For example, the following primary colors, when mixed in equal amounts, produce secondary colors: red and yellow make orange, blue and yellow make green, and red and blue make purple. (All colors combined make black.)

In Living Color

WHAT COLOR IS BLACK?

Purpose
To demonstrate paper chromatography.

Curriculum
Chemistry and chromatography

Requirements
Time: 15 minutes   *Difficulty Level: 3*

Materials
- water-soluble, black felt tip marker
- coffee filters or paper towels
- cup
- water
- scissors

Directions
1. Cut a strip of coffee filter material or a paper towel into about 1-inch wide and about 1–2 inches longer than your cup.
2. With the marker, draw a horizontal line across the strip about 1 inch from the bottom.
3. Fill the cup with about 1 inch of water.
4. Place the strip in the water so that the bottom of the strip just touches the water. The ink line must be above the water level. Rest the top of the strip over the edge of the cup.
5. Observe the movement of the water and color until the color band spreads up the strip of paper. This should take about 5–10 minutes.
6. Remove the strip and allow it to dry.

Explanation
This experiment demonstrates chromatography, a process by which the components of a liquid are absorbed by the paper at different rates. The liquid begins to move the components of the ink outward at different rates of speed along the porous paper. The ink molecules interact less strongly with the paper and more strongly with the liquid being drawn up into the paper. The result is that the colors that make up the ink separate into different color bands. The movement of liquid through paper in this activity is an example of capillary action. Capillary action is a physical effect caused by the interactions of a liquid with the walls of a thin tube.

Variation
Try using different types of papers, and different colors of water-soluble felt tip markers.

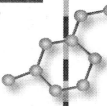

SOMEWHERE OVER THE RAINBOW

Purpose

To demonstrate the force of adhesion.

Curriculum

Force of adhesion

Requirements

Time: 15 minutes   *Difficulty Level:* 3

Materials

- vegetable oil
- several drinking straws
- pencil
- paper or card
- flat aluminum pie dish
- several colors of oil-based paint
- masking tape
- water

Directions

1. Lightly oil the inside surface of the aluminum pie tin.
2. Fill the tin with about ½ inch of water.
3. Pick up a small amount of paint with a straw by dipping the end of the straw into the paint, keeping a finger over the other end of the straw. Lift the finger when the straw is above the water.
4. Place two drops of the paint on the water.
5. Gently stir the paint into any shape with the pencil point.
6. Use a different straw for each of the paints; add dots of color to the tin of water.
7. Swirl each color as you add paint or gently blow through the straw for a different effect. (Do not inhale through the straw.)
8. Fasten masking tape loops about 1–2 inches in diameter to the back of your paper or index card.
9. Lift the paper by the loops and gently lay it down on the water.
10. Wait 3 seconds and pick the paper up by the loops.
11. Let the paper dry.

Explanation

The colors of your paint were attracted to the paper due to the force of adhesion. Adhesion is the active force that works when two different substances are brought in contact with one. The paint remains on the surface of the water because it is oil-based and oil is less dense than water.

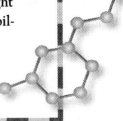

SPINSATIONAL COLOR DISK

Purpose

To visualize the nature of color.

Curriculum

Light reflection and optics

Requirements

Time: 15 minutes   *Difficulty Level:* 4

Materials

Part A:

- cardboard
- scissors
- black pen
- black marker
- glue stick
- piece of white unlined paper
- drawing compass
- ruler

Part B:

- hammer
- long finishing nail
- 3–5-inch piece of 2-inch × 4-inch (or similar size piece of wood)

Directions

Part A:

1. Using the compass, draw a circle with a 4-inch diameter on the cardboard. *Note:* That would be the 2-inch mark on the compass itself.
2. Cut out the cardboard circle.
3. Use the sharp end of the compass or a pencil point; punch a small hole in the center of the cardboard.
4. Glue your cardboard circle or wheel on top of the white unlined paper.
5. Cut the paper to the size of the wheel.
6. Using the ruler and black pen, divide the paper side of the wheel into eight even sections.
7. With the black marker, draw different designs and shapes in the sections.

Part B:

1. Pound the nail in the center of the wood. The nail should protrude out of the opposite end of the wood at least ¾ inch or longer.
2. Put the nail through the hole in your wheel.
3. Spin the circle around a few times and vary the speed.
4. Stare directly at the wheel as you spin it.

Safety Note: Be careful that no one is injured with the protruding end of the nail.

Explanation

The white spaces on the wheel or disk reflect all of the colors of the rainbow. Each white space is only seen for a short amount of time because it is followed by a black space. With these varying the lengths of black and white, the eye (the brain) will record only certain colors. When the disk slows down, you can see more of the colors because you have more time to see the white spaces.

In Living Color

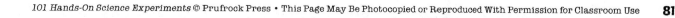

THE CRYSTAL GARDEN

Purpose

To demonstrate the process of evaporation and crystallization.

Curriculum

Crystal formation and evaporation

Requirements

Time: 10 minutes (plus 24-hour drying time)   *Difficulty Level:* 4

Materials

- pie pan (ceramic or aluminum)
- 8–10 pieces of charcoal (Note: Do not use charcoal that is treated with lighter fluid.)
- 2–4 tablespoons each of water, salt, and ammonia
- 4 tablespoons of bluing (available in the laundry section of most supermarkets)
- mixing bowl
- food coloring of various colors

Directions

1. Cover the bottom of the pie pan with the charcoal.
2. Mix the water, salt, bluing, and ammonia together in the mixing bowl.
3. Carefully pour the mixture over the charcoal, making sure that all the charcoal pieces get wet.
4. Squirt a few drops of various shades of food coloring on the charcoal.
5. Set the pie pan aside in an undisturbed, airy place for 24 hours.
6. Observe and discuss the colorful, flower-like growth (the crystallization) that occurs.

Safety Note: If you tell students to experiment with a different variable in this activity, caution them never to use bleach with ammonia, as the result will produce poisonous gases.

Explanation

The salt crystal garden is formed by the recrystallization of salt. As the water evaporates, including the water in the bluing (a colloidal suspension of iron, carbon, and nitrogen molecules), the blue particles can no longer be supported and the excess salt dries out. The salt crystallizes around the bluing particles. The ammonia starts to break down the charcoal into a liquid, aiding the evaporation process. The remaining charcoal soaks up the additional moisture until it is completely saturated. As the liquid evaporates, the salt solution begins to dry and recrystallizes in the new forms.

Variation

Other porous materials can be used as the base of the garden, such as a piece of porous brick or a sponge.

In Living Color

WE EAT AND DRINK ACIDS AND BASES

Purpose

To illustrate acids and bases that are commonly found in kitchens.

Curriculum

Acids and bases; chemical reactions

Requirements

Time: 15 minutes   *Difficulty Level:* 4

Materials

- 1 tablespoon of each of these common acids: lemon juice, orange juice, vitamin C tablets (pulverized), soda, and vinegar
- 1 tablespoon each of these common bases: baking soda, liquid antacid, ammonia (or ammonia based glass cleaner), and egg whites
- small amounts of natural indicators: red cabbage, red apple skin, cherries, beets, and grape juice
- knife (to chop up natural indicators)   •   hot water
- 12 or more small jars   •   strainer

Directions

1. Using your knife, prepare the natural indicators by chopping the materials into small bits. Then, pour hot water over the materials. Strain off the solid material and store the remaining indicator solution in its own jar. The liquid solution can be diluted, using equal parts of water, to create more liquid indicator.
2. In each of the jars, place 1 tablespoon of one of the indicator solution. The first jar should be your control (used for color comparison). Add nothing to this jar.
3. Add 1 tablespoon of lemon juice to the second jar. Add other acids to the other jars, keeping track of the color changes.
4. Add the common bases to the next 4 jars.
5. Repeat experiment with other natural indicators.

Explanation

The color change is a chemical reaction. Indicators show pH level, that is, how acidic or basic a material is. When using a cabbage indicator in this activity, for instance, note that a resulting pink color range indicates acidic quality; a blue/green/violet color range indicates a basic quality. pH levels range from 1–14 (strong acid to strong base).

Variation

Have students work with pH test paper strips or litmus paper, available in science supply stores or drugstores, to extend their experience with pH testing.

In Living Color

Our Good Green Earth

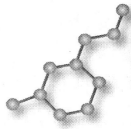

Next time you take a breath of fresh air, thank a plant. Explain to students that plants are machines of nature that take in the carbon dioxide that animals (including humans) exhale, and then turn the carbon dioxide into breathable oxygen. This process is called photosynthesis. The abundance of plants on Earth is endless. After exploring the scientific aspects of plant life in the following experiments, you may want to consider taking your students on a class excursion or two to an arboretum, nature center, garden, forest preserve, or conservatory. This is a great way to expand the walls of your classroom and give your students a rewarding experience.

CELERY STALKER 86
MATH . . . FOR TREES 87
ORANGE YOU GLAD 88
POPCORN PUSH-UPS 89
SOUR APPLE JUICE 90
WATER LILIES 91
YOU'RE ALL WET 92
GIMME' SOME AIR 93
PINECONE PIXIES 94
DON'T CRY FOR THESE CELLS 95
DOWN THEY GO 96
I'M CRACKIN' UP 97
CHLOROPHYLL CAPERS 98

CELERY STALKER

Purpose
To illustrate how plants absorb water and food.

Curriculum
Osmosis

Requirements
Time: 2 minutes plus observation time   *Difficulty Level:* 1

Materials
- stalk of celery with its leaves
- glass of water
- red food coloring
- bright light
- tablespoon measurer

Directions
1. Mix about 1 tablespoon of red food coloring into the glass of water.
2. Place the stalk of celery into the glass.
3. Place it in a bright light and let it remain overnight.

Explanation
The leaves turn reddish color. The celery stalk is the stem of the celery. This stalk absorbs water and minerals from the soil through its root hairs by a process called osmosis. Osmosis is a process by which some liquids and gases pass through a skin-like membrane. Water passes into all cells and is carried up through its center tubes to the plant's stems and leaves.

Variation
Repeat this experiment with other vegetables.

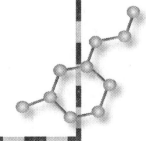

MATH . . . FOR TREES

Purpose

To determine how to calculate the age of a tree.

Curriculum

Math; botany

Requirements

Time: 5 minutes   *Difficulty Level:* 1

Materials

- several different nonevergreen trees
- tape measure (in inches)

Directions

1. Hold the tape measure about 3 feet above the ground and measure the distance around the tree.
2. This is the approximate age of the tree, in years. Discuss what causes trees to grow at different rates—how accurate is your estimation of the tree's age?

Explanation

By measuring around the trunk of a tree, you can get an estimate of its age. Trees grow at different rates depending on amount of water, drainage, and weather conditions. The circumference (distance around the tree) of a mature tree increases about 1 inch every year. Palm trees and some fast-growing trees, such as conifers, do not follow this guide.

ORANGE YOU GLAD

Purpose

To determine the differing sugar contents of a single orange.

Curriculum

Fruit growth

Requirements

Time: 2 minutes   *Difficulty Level:* 1

Materials

- orange
- knife

Directions

1. Peel the orange.
2. Carefully cut one slice across the stem and then one slice across the blossom end.
3. Taste them.

Explanation

The blossom end of the orange is sweeter because it develops more sugar due to its increased exposure to the sun. For this reason, fruits grown in the temperate zone are only 10–15% sugar while those from the tropics, such as bananas, figs and dates, are about 20–60% sugar.

Variation

Try this activity with other fruits.

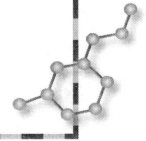

POPCORN PUSH-UPS

Purpose
To observe how popcorn seeds absorb water.

Curriculum
Water pressure

Requirements
Time: 2 minutes (plus overnight wait time) *Difficulty Level:* 1

Materials
- bag of unpopped popcorn kernels
- clear jar
- plastic
- dish
- water

Directions
1. Fill the jar with the popcorn kernels.
2. Fill the jar with water.
3. Place the dish over the top of the jar.
4. Check back in an hour and then again the next day.

Explanation
The popcorn kernels, now bloated with water, expanded and pushed the dish off the lid of the jar. In nature, seeds are weigh-lifters, too. When a seed swells with water, pressure builds on it. The seeds push aside soil, making room for the baby plant's root and stem. When you pop popcorn, the same principle applies. The popcorn absorbs moisture and then explodes to make the full kernel of popped corn.

Our Good Green Earth

SOUR APPLE JUICE

Purpose

To tests how apple juice changes into vinegar.

Curriculum

Chemical change

Requirements

Time: 1 minute (plus several days for observation and testing)   *Difficulty Level:* 1

Materials

- 8 ounce glass of apple juice
- glass
- small clear jar
- baking soda
- tablespoon measurer

Directions

1. Pour the apple juice into a glass and allow it to sit undisturbed for several days.
2. Each day test the apple juice by removing 2–3 tablespoons of the juice and placing it into the small jar.
3. Add a pinch of baking soda to the jar. If bubbles form, vinegar is present.

Explanation

The bubbling of the baking soda with the old apple juice means you no longer have apple juice. You have acetic acid or vinegar. Some companies use apple juice to make vinegar. Small growing microbes can change the sugar in apple juice turn into vinegar. This is a chemical reaction that produces carbon dioxide gas, which is the foam you observed.

Variation

Try this experiment with other type of fruit juices.

WATER LILIES

Purpose

To display how water moves through plant vascular tissue.

Curriculum

Capillary action and physics

Requirements

Time: 5 minutes   *Difficulty Level:* 1

Materials

- sheet of plain paper
- scissors
- crayons or colored pencils
- bowl of water

Directions

1. Draw a large-sized lily with at least 10 long-sized petals protruding from the center of the flower.
2. Using your crayons or colored pencils, color your flower.
3. Cut out the flower along the solid lines.
4. Using your fingers, fold the paper petals firmly into the center.
5. Place the lily on the water and observe.

Explanation

The petals of the lily slowly open. These papers consist mostly of plant fibers that are made of very small capillary tubes. As the water rises in these tubes, it causes the paper to swell and the petals to open.

Our Good Green Earth

YOU'RE ALL WET

Purpose

To demonstrates how overwatering plants can be a problem.

Curriculum

Osmosis

Requirements

Time: 1 minute (plus overnight observation)   *Difficulty Level:* 1

Materials

- fresh rhubarb stalks (found in the produce section of grocery store)
- bowl of water
- undisturbed place

Directions

1. Place several stalks of rhubarb in the bowl of water.
2. Leave the rhubarb undisturbed for 1 day.
3. Discuss observations.

Explanation

The ends of the stalks are split and curly. Rhubarb stalks contain cells that absorb water at different rates. Some of these cells absorb more water than others, causing them to swell open and split apart. Many plants have these special types of cells. This is the reason behind why you never want to overwater a plant. Too much water, like too little water, can destroy the cell structure and kill the plant.

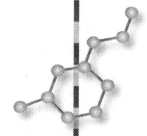

GIMME' SOME AIR

Purpose
To demonstrate the process of photosynthesis.

Curriculum
Photosynthesis

Requirements
Time: 2 minutes (plus several hours wait time) *Difficulty Level:* 2

Materials
- clear bowl
- clear jar that fits inside the bowl
- several weeds or plants from a pond or lake
- water
- a sunny location

Directions
1. Fill the bowl about ½-way with water.
2. Place the plants in the bowl of water.
3. Invert the jar, and place it over the plants in the bowl.
4. Push the plants into the jar, and then rest the jar on the bottom of the bowl. The plants should be covered by water in the inverted jar.
5. Leave the bowl in bright sunlight for several hours.
6. Discuss observations.

Explanation
Bubbles of oxygen start to rise to the water surface. Plants give off oxygen in a complex process called photosynthesis. This takes place in the green portion of the plant. All plants use this process to release oxygen into the environment. All animals, including humans, use this oxygen to breathe.

Variation
Try this with other plant such a flowers or grass clippings.

Our Good Green Earth

PINECONE PIXIES

Purpose

To determine if pinecones contain seeds.

Curriculum

Botany

Requirements

Time: 5 minutes   *Difficulty Level:* 2

Materials

- several young evergreen pinecones (cones with tightly closed scales)
- clean towel or rag
- sheet of newsprint

Directions

1. Spread out the newspaper on a flat surface.
2. Wrap the towel around the end of one of the pinecones.
3. While holding the towel in your hand, twist the cone back and forth several times to loosen its scales. If this is too difficult, soak the cones in water for a few hours.
4. While holding the base of the cone with the towel with one hand, use your fingers of the other hand to pull out several scales near the tip of the cone.

Explanation

Two seeds, each attached to a paper-like wing, are found on the inside of the scales of the pinecone. Pinecones contain seeds of a pine tree. Pine trees are conifers, which are nonflowering plants that reproduce by forming cones. Most conifers are evergreens, that is, that their leaves stay green on the trees all year.

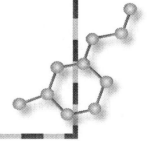

Our Good Green Earth

DON'T CRY FOR THESE CELLS

Purpose

To observe the cell structures of an onion.

Curriculum

Cell structure and botany

Requirements

Time: 5 minutes   *Difficulty Level:* 3

Materials

- fresh onion
- magnifying glass
- knife
- tweezers
- clean windowpane of glass

Directions

1. Remove the top dried, brownish skin section of the onion and then carefully cut a small square section out of the body of the onion.
2. Use the tweezers and gently pull away a thin film of onionskin.
3. Press the onionskin onto a windowpane so it sticks in position.
4. Observe the skin through your magnifying glass. Discuss.

Explanation

You should be able to see rectangular-shaped cells. Plant cells are not the same as animal cells. Animal cells are soft and flexible. Plant cells have a tough outer wall that gives them a fixed round shape. Plant cells are usually much larger than animal cells, which makes them easier to see.

Variation

Using an eyedropper, place a drop or two of iodine tincture on your slide. This will enhance the structure of the onion and make the cells easier to observe.

Our Good Green Earth

DOWN THEY GO

Purpose

To observe plant root pattern formations.

Curriculum

Plant germination and botany

Requirements

Time: 10 minutes (plus several days to germinate)   *Difficulty Level:* 3

Materials

- flat Styrofoam food container
- wet paper towels
- six fresh popcorn kernels
- plastic wrap

Directions

1. Lay several wet paper towels on the food container.
2. Spread the popcorn kernels with their roots (the pointed end) facing the same direction.
3. Tightly seal the entire container with the plastic wrap so no water can leak out.
4. Stand the container on its edge so the pointed ends of the kernels are pointing down.
5. Allow them to grow for several days and notice how the roots are growing.
6. Turn the container 90° every 2–3 days and observe. Do this several times.

Explanation

No matter what direction you turn the seeds, they always turn downward. After a week or so, the roots make an interesting pattern. When a seedling grows in soil, its roots go downward. If an object is in its way, the seed roots move around it, and keep on going down—even if you point the roots up, they turn back.

Variation

Try this with other dried seeds.

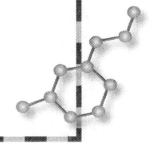

I'M CRACKIN' UP

Purpose

To discover the strength of a plant root system.

Curriculum

Botany and root development

Requirements

Time: 10 minutes (plus several days germination time) *Difficulty Level:* 3

Materials

- potting soil
- several raw eggs and the egg carton
- marigold flower seeds
- small spoon
- water
- sunny environment

Directions

1. Carefully crack an egg from the top, dispose of the insides, and peel back the eggshell so you have a half eggshell.
2. Gently using the spoon, fill the half eggshell to the top with the soil. Do this with several eggshells if you wish.
3. Place the eggshell back into the egg carton.
4. Sprinkle seeds on the top and cover them with a little soil.
5. Place them in a warm, light location and water every day. Do not overwater.
6. After the seeds start to germinate, lift your eggshell flowerpot and observe the bottom of the plant.

Explanation

The root system has forced and broke its way through the bottom of the eggshell. Some roots are so strong that they can even push through cracks in rock. Try this activity other plant seeds.

CHLOROPHYLL CAPERS

Purpose
To demonstrate that plants contain chlorophyll.

Curriculum
Chemical extractions

Requirements
Time: 15 minutes　　　　　　*Difficulty Level:* 4

Materials
- 7–10 spinach leaves
- 2 cups water
- stove
- saucepan or pot
- slotted spoon
- clear glass

Directions
1. Heat the water in the pan until it comes to a boil.
2. With your spoon, place the spinach leaves in the pot and carefully pour in the boiling water.
3. Continue heating until you notice the water turning green.
4. Remove the pot from the stove and allow for cooling of the liquid.
5. Carefully remove the spinach from the pot.
6. Pour the water into the glass and observe the color.

Safety Note: An adult needs to supervise this activity to avoid spilling the boiling water.

Explanation
The green color you extracted from the leaves is a substance called chlorophyll. Chlorophyll is a green substance found in plants that captures light that is necessary for triggering chemical reactions in the process of photosynthesis.

Variation
Repeat this experiment with other green plants. Try using a white flower and/or other food coloring.

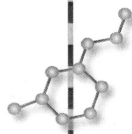

Our Good Green Earth

Creepy Crawlers

Your students may not be accustomed to thinking of insects as animals, but not only are they animals—they are the most numerous animal on Earth. About 85% of the (approximately) 1 million identified animal species have been recognized as insects. At any one time on Earth, there are estimated to be about 200 million insects for every living person. A ratio of 200,000,000 to 1 is pretty impressive. Explain to students that it is estimated that there are about 26 billion insects living in each square mile of habitable land. In fact, the combined weight of all insects on Earth exceeds the weight of all other terrestrial animals! If there is one topic that really turns kids on to hands-on science, it is insects. In this section of activities, you and your students will really get "bugged."

HEADS OR TAILS? 100
NOISY BUGS 101
SPIDER TENSION 102
THE EYES HAVE IT 103
CANDY BUGS YOU CAN EAT 104
HOW FLIES EAT 105
SPIDER ART 106
AT A SNAIL'S PACE 107
THE WORMS MOVE IN, THE WORMS MOVE OUT 108
ANTS IN YOUR PANTS 109

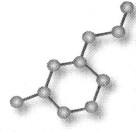

HEADS OR TAILS?

Purpose

To determine which is the head and tail of an earthworm.

Curriculum

Entomology and anatomy

Requirements

Time: 1 minute   *Difficulty Level:* 1

Materials

- a long earthworm
- plate
- pencil
- water

Directions

1. Rinse the plate to make it wet.
2. Gently place the earthworm on the plate.
3. With the pencil, lightly touch one end of the worm.
4. Immediately touch the other end.
5. Discuss your observations, allowing students to guess which end is the head or tail of the earthworm.

Safety Note: Wash you hands before and after touching the worms. Do not poke at the worms excessively. Return the worm outside after experiment is concluded.

Explanation

The side that moves the quickest is the tail because a worm's tail is extremely sensitive to touch. If a bird touches a worm's tail, the worm will suddenly contract and pull its whole body underground in order to escape. When you touch the head the worm, the reaction time is much slower.

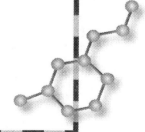

NOISY BUGS

Purpose

To demonstrate how some types of insects make noise.

Curriculum

Sound waves and motion

Requirements

Time: 1 minute   *Difficulty Level:* 1

Materials

- a fingernail file or emery board
- index card (any size)

Directions

1. Hold the index card upright with one long edge resting on a table.
2. Support the card with one hand as you draw the rough side of the file across the card quickly several times.
3. Discuss your observations.

Explanation

The vibrations between the file and the card should cause a rasping sound. Certain insects, like crickets and grasshoppers, produce sounds in much the same way. The motion of certain body parts causes the formation of sound waves. These insects make sounds by rubbing two body parts against each other.

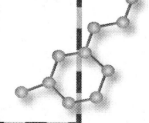

SPIDER TENSION

Purpose

To determine how a spider senses vibrations in its web.

Curriculum

Physics and motion

Requirements

Time: 1 minute   *Difficulty Level:* 1

Materials

- a long piece of string
- two stationary objects (a table leg and a door)
- a partner

Directions

1. Stretch the string tightly between the two stationary objects.
2. At one end of the string, gently place the tips of your fingers on the top of the string.
3. While you are looking the other way, have your partner pluck the opposite end of the string, starting off by lightly plucking the string and then firmly pulling on the string.
4. Switch roles with your partner and then discuss your observations.

Explanation

You should be able to feel the varying degrees of vibration on your end of the string. A gentle or firm touch produces a different strength of vibration. Spiders feel the vibrations in much the same way in their webs. These webs act like telegraph lines—when the web shakes; the spider senses the movement with sensors on its legs.

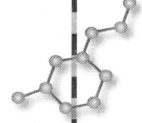

THE EYES HAVE IT

Purpose

To illustrate how compound vision eyes work.

Curriculum

Sight and motion

Requirements

Time: 5 minutes   *Difficulty Level:* 1

Materials

- 25–30 drinking straws
- moving fan (with blades covered so fingers cannot get inside)
- tape

Directions

1. Stand the straws upright and secure several strips of tape around them to make one large tube. This is a model of an insect's compound eye.
2. Close one eye and look through one end of the straw at a stationary object.
3. Now look at a moving fan.
4. Make a second straw eye and look through the "insect's eyes" at the same time.

Explanation

Grasshoppers (and many other insects) have two large eyes called compound eyes, one on each side of their head. The eyes are made up of thousands of separate units called ommatidia; the surface of each lens is called a facet. Scientists do not fully understand how insects actually see objects, however, your straw model gives you an example of how certain insects' sight is different from humans.

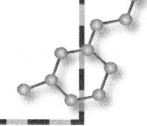

CANDY BUGS YOU CAN EAT

Purpose

To make a model of an adult insect's three main body parts.

Curriculum

Entomology and anatomy

Requirements

Time: 10 minutes   *Difficulty Level:* 2

Materials

- six gumdrops
- 12 round toothpicks

Directions

1. Place three gumdrops on one toothpick. This is your insect's abdomen.
2. Place two gumdrops on another toothpick. This is your insect's thorax.
3. Push the gumdrops firmly against each other and break off any part of the toothpick that is sticking out.
4. Attach a single gumdrop (the insect's head) to the thorax with a toothpick.
5. Then, attach the thorax to the abdomen with another toothpick.
6. Place three toothpicks at an angle sticking down opposite each other in the thorax and four toothpicks, set opposite each other in the abdomen. These are your insect's legs.
7. Position your insect so it is standing on all six legs.
8. Break a toothpick in half and use them as the antenna on the insect's head.
9. Discuss the different body parts of an insect, and each body part's importance.

Explanation

An adult insect is divided into three main body parts, the head, thorax, and abdomen. The head bears the eyes (usually a pair of compound eyes), the antennae, and the mouthparts. The thorax is in the middle, and it is composed of three segments. It bears three pairs of legs (one on each segment) and usually two pairs of wings. Some insects have only one pair of wings. Finally, the abdomen takes up the rear, which is composed of 11 segments. The abdomen bears the external genitalia of the insect. The abdomen is divided into even smaller segments, just like your gumdrop model. All insects have six legs.

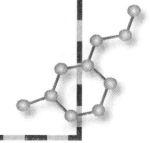

HOW FLIES EAT

Purpose

To demonstrate how flies consume their food.

Curriculum

Entomology and digestion

Requirements

Time: 5 minutes (plus 24-hour setup)   *Difficulty Level:* 2

Materials

- a jar of sweet potato baby food
- eyedropper
- masking tape
- pen
- your saliva
- refrigerator

Directions

1. Try to suck up the baby food with the eyedropper. You shouldn't be able to do this, as the baby food is too thick to suck into the eyedropper. Wash the dropper.
2. Collect as much saliva in your mouth as possible and spit the saliva onto the surface of the sweet potatoes.
3. Close the baby food jar.
4. Place the jar in the refrigerator and leave it undisturbed for 24 hours.
5. Remove the jar and repeat Step 1.
6. Compare the outcomes of both attempts to suck baby food into the eyedropper.

Explanation

At first, you were unable to draw any of the sweet potatoes into the eyedropper because the baby food was too thick. However, after the saliva was in the jar for 24 hours, the food became thinner and it was easily drawn into the dropper. Human saliva, like the saliva of flies (and many other insects) contains a chemical digestive enzyme called amylase. This breaks down starch (a complex chemical found in many foods) into simpler materials. Digestive enzymes are enzymes that help break down the complex components of the foods we eat.

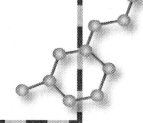

SPIDER ART

Purpose

To display the intricacies of a spider web.

Curriculum

Habitation and environment

Requirements

Time: 5 minutes   *Difficulty Level:* 2

Materials

- an aerosol can of hairspray
- abandoned spider web
- sheet of cardboard

Directions

1. Find an abandoned spider web.
2. Gently spray the entire web with aerosol hairspray.
3. Spray the cardboard with the hairspray.
4. Quickly press the wet cardboard against the web and pull it away.
5. Allow the web and cardboard to dry.
6. Show the web to students and discuss.

Explanation

Hairspray is a sticky substance that caused the web, which consists of pure silk, to stick to the cardboard, preserving the pattern of the carefully woven web. Observe the detailed patterns of the web. Do you see any identical patterns? Have students draw the web's patterns on a sheet of paper.

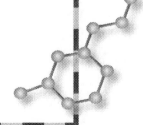

AT A SNAIL'S PACE

Purpose
To study the movement of snails.

Curriculum
Entomology

Requirements
Time: 10 minutes (plus additional observation time)   *Difficulty Level:* 3

Materials
- several snails (purchased from local pet shop or collected from a garden)
- large clay flowerpot or other similar object
- enamel paint
- thin paintbrush
- water
- paper towels

Directions
1. Pick up a snail and tap it to make it pull inside its body.
2. Paint a number on each snail's back, starting with one. Be careful not to get any paint on the snail's soft body.
3. Lay the flowerpot on its side.
4. Place a wet paper towel at the bottom of the pot.
5. Place all of the snails on the ground at the edge of the flowerpot and observe their movement for a short time.
6. Observe the snails again after 30 minutes.
7. Repeat Steps 3 and 5 without the wet towel.
8. Discuss how the movement patterns of the snails have changed with the change in setting.

Safety Note: Wash your hands before and after handling the snails. When completed with the activity, return the snails to your garden or other moist, outdoor location.

Explanation
Snails are slow-moving animals that like to rest in damp places. Observe them for a while and see how far they move. Compare how long it takes the snails to move with and without the wet towel at the bottom of the pot. You may notice that the snails move in a random pattern, and do not necessary follow a straight path.

THE WORMS MOVE IN, THE WORMS MOVE OUT

Purpose

To observe the preferred environment of earthworms.

Curriculum

Light sensitivity

Requirements

Time: 20 minutes (plus several weeks of observation time)   *Difficulty Level:* 3

Materials

- 2 cups of dark-colored soil
- 1 tablespoon of dried oats
- large bowl
- spoon
- rubber band
- 5–8 earthworms (purchased or found outdoors)
- 1 cup of light-colored sand
- dark-colored construction paper
- water
- quart-sized, wide-mouthed jar
- cool location

Directions

1. Pour the soil in the bowl, and add water to moisten the soil.
2. Pour half of the moistened soil into the jar.
3. Pour the sand over the soil as the second layer in the jar.
4. Add the remaining soil to the jar.
5. Sprinkle the oats over the soil in the jar.
6. Gently place the worms in the jar.
7. Wrap the paper around the jar and secure it with the rubber band. Place in a cool location.
8. Every day for several weeks, remove the paper and observe the jar. After observing, put the paper back around the jar and return the jar to the cool location.
9. Discuss your observations. Have students take notes to keep track of the weekly changes.

Explanation

After placing the worms in the jar, the worms will start wiggling and eventually burrow into the soil. After a few days, tunnels should be seen in the soil as the dark soil and light sand become mixed. Worms live and eat their way through soil. They get nourishment from the remains of other living organisms that live in the soil. Worms move about and loosen soil so that water and air needed by plants can easily pass through the dense ground.

ANTS IN YOUR PANTS

Purpose

To observe an ant colony.

Curriculum

Entomology

Requirements

Time: 20 minutes (plus several weeks of observation time)   *Difficulty Level:* 4

Materials

- 2 cups of very fine soil
- long-handled mixing spoon
- apple wedge
- rubber band and tape
- black construction paper
- a cool area
- quart-sized wide-mouthed jar
- cotton ball moistened with tap water
- 6-inch × 6-inch square cloth
- scissors
- 25–30 ants (from an outdoor anthill)

Directions

1. Pour the soil into the jar.
2. Locate an anthill and then use the long-handled mixing spoon to stir up the top of an anthill. When the ants run out, scoop up a few dozen of them and place them into the jar.
3. Quickly moisten the cotton ball and drop it into the jar along with the apple. Immediately cover the jar with the cloth. Use the rubber band to secure the cloth to the jar.
4. Cut the construction paper to make a tube that fits loosely around the outside of the jar. The tube should be about 2 inches higher than the soil inside the jar.
5. Place your ant colony in a cool, dry area.
6. Several times a day for about a week, slide the tube off the jar and observe.
7. Discuss the changes occurring in the jar with your class. (See Explanation for details.)

Safety Note: Use special care when working with ants. Do not allow them to get on your skin. Do not do this experiment if you are allergic to ants. Use only small ants that you observe in your yard or sidewalk. Do not pick up red ants. Make sure to wash your hands after handling the ants.

Explanation

At first, the ants frantically ran around the jar before they settled down. Some should begin digging almost immediately. By the end of the week, clearly defined tunnels are visible in the soil and small anthills should dot the surface. Ants are insects that live in organized colonies. Observe your ant colony for an extended period of time to watch this colony develop.

Kitchen Science

When your students go into their kitchen, it is unlikely that they think of science. After you and your students try out these exciting kitchen-oriented activities, they will have a whole new perspective on kitchen-related products. Using items ranging from eggs to lemons and fruit juice to mousse, your students are going to get very hungry—hungry for science, that is.

BUTTER BEATERS 112
POTATO POWER 113
HOW NOW BROWN COW! 114
LEMON BATTERY 115
INVISIBLE FRUIT INK 116
MARSHMALLOW GLACIERS 117
THIS IS NUTS! 118
EGG POWER 119
INSTANT MOUSSE 120
I SCREAM, YOU SCREAM, WE ALL SCREAM FOR ICE CREAM 121
YEAST BEASTS 122

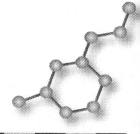

BUTTER BEATERS

Purpose
To demonstrate the creation of butter from cream.

Curriculum
Mixtures and solutions

Requirements
Time: 5 minutes   *Difficulty Level:* 1

Materials
- several small marbles
- small glass jar with lid
- heavy whipping cream (or instant pudding mix)

Directions
1. Fill the jar half full with the whipping cream.
2. Place the marbles into the jar and secure the lid.
3. Carefully shake the container for several minutes.
4. Discuss what's taking place inside the jar, taking note of the chemical transitions.

Safety Note: Students should not eat this butter unless they are working with very clean equipment and fresh whipping cream.

Explanation
By shaking the jar, the marbles hit the fat molecules in the whipping cream, resulting in agitation. This agitation causes the particles in the cream to separate and mix with the air particles. This results in the formation of butter.

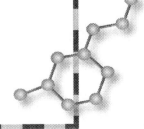

POTATO POWER

Purpose
To illustrate the power of air pressure.

Curriculum
Force and air pressure

Requirements
Time: 1 minute   *Difficulty Level:* 1

Materials
- small, uncooked, and unpeeled potato
- plastic drinking straw (not the flex-type)

Directions
1. Hold the straw by its center and try to jab it through your potato.
2. Now cover one end of the straw with your finger and try to stick the straw through the potato. Use a quick, steady jab.
3. Discuss why you were able to puncture the potato using the second method.

Explanation
The straw will pierce the potato only when one end of the straw is closed up—that is, when your finger traps a volume of air inside the straw. This trapped air is strong enough (along with the force you place on the straw) to allow you to pierce the potato.

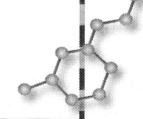

HOW NOW BROWN COW!

Kitchen Science

Purpose

To demonstrate how milk can be separated into its solid and liquid parts.

Curriculum

Mixtures, solutions, and chemical reactions

Requirements

Time: **3 minutes**   *Difficulty Level:* 1

Materials

- small jar with a lid
- fresh milk
- 2 tablespoons of vinegar

Directions

1. Fill the jar ¾ full of milk.
2. Add 2 tablespoons of vinegar.
3. Allow the jar to sit for a few minutes.
4. Discuss why the particles in the milk separate.

Explanation

The solid particles in the milk are evenly spread throughout the liquid. The vinegar, which is a weak acid, causes the small, undissolved particles to clump together, forming the solid curd. The liquid that remains is called the whey. Milk is an example of a colloid, which is a mixture of liquids and small particles.

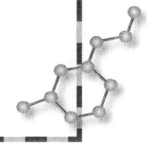

LEMON BATTERY

Purpose

To illustrate how a battery works.

Curriculum

Electricity and power

Requirements

Time: 5 minutes   *Difficulty Level:* 1

Materials

- a small lemon
- piece of noninsulated copper wire
- wire cutters
- paper clip

Directions

1. Straighten out the paper clip and copper wire. They should be the same lengths. Trim, if necessary.
2. Stick both wires deep into the lemon, side by side, about ½ inch apart.
3. Gently place the free ends of the wires on your tongue.
4. Discuss the reaction occurring.

Safety Note: Warn students they will feel a tingling sensation on their tongues. Each student should have his or her own "lemon battery."

Explanation

Students should have received a slight tingle on their tongue from the homemade lemon battery because electrons (negatively charged particles that make up electricity) passed through their saliva onto their tongue. The citric acid (or juice) in the lemon acted as a conductor of electricity. For the lemon battery to complete the circuit, which it did when they felt the tingling sensation on their tongues, two different types of conductive metals (in this case, copper and steel alloy) are needed.

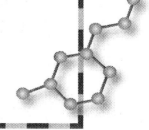

INVISIBLE FRUIT INK

Purpose

To demonstrate how a fruit juice breaks down chemically.

Curriculum

Decomposition

Requirements

Time: 3 minutes (plus drying time)   *Difficulty Level:* 2

Materials

- any type of fruit juice
- paintbrush with a fine tip
- plastic cup
- notebook paper
- lamp with a 75-watt (or greater) light bulb

Directions

1. Place a small amount of juice in the plastic cup.
2. Dip the paintbrush in the juice. Use your brush to write a secret message on a piece of notebook paper.
3. Allow the paper and "ink" to dry (about 20 minutes).
4. Turn on the lamp, and hold the paper over the light bulb until the message is readable.
5. Discuss why the message is visible to the eye, and point out the change in color.

Safety Note: Do not touch the light bulb and do not leave the paper on the light bulb.

Explanation

When the juice is heated, the once-living plant materials that make up the beverage break down, producing (among other things) carbon, which is black. Carbon is a basic element that is in all living things, including our bodies. The decomposition of the fruit juice ink makes the writing visible even after drying.

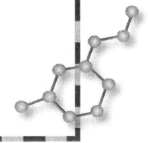

Kitchen Science

MARSHMALLOW GLACIERS

Purpose
To demonstrate how pressure increases compaction.

Curriculum
Glacier formation and pressure

Requirements
Time: 5 minutes   *Difficulty Level:* 2

Materials
- a thick, tall, clear plastic glass
- 6–8 regular-sized marshmallows
- small piece of cardboard
- small set of weights
- scissors

Directions
1. Stack the marshmallows in the plastic glass.
2. Cut out a cardboard disc to fit snugly inside the glass.
3. Place the cardboard disc on top of the marshmallows.
4. Place the weights, one at a time, on top of the disc.
5. Discuss the appearance of the marshmallows at the top and bottom of the glass. Talk about how this is similar to glacier formation.

Explanation
As the marshmallows start to push together, the lower layers are more compact due the additional weight on them. This is similar to the compaction and pressure of snow forming on a glacier. A glacier is a slow-moving body of ice found in polar climates. As snow falls, the bottom layers of the glacier have more weight on them and turn to ice. The additional weight adds pressure; therefore, the bottom layers of the glacier are more compacted than the top layers.

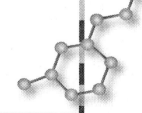

THIS IS NUTS!

Purpose
To demonstrate that matter cannot occupy the same space at the same time.

Curriculum
Molecular motion

Requirements
Time: 3 minutes   *Difficulty Level:* 2

Materials
- 1-quart glass jar with a lid
- uncooked rice
- whole walnut (in shell)

Directions
1. Fill the jar ¾ full with uncooked rice.
2. Place the walnut on top of the rice and close the lid.
3. Hold the jar upright, and then turn it over.
4. Shake the jar back and forth (sideways) vigorously, until the walnut surfaces on the other side. Do not shake up and down.

Explanation
Inside the jar there are spaces between the grains of rice. As the jar is shaken, the grains of rice settle and compact in the jar. When the rice vibrates and pushes the rice kernels together, this in turn forces the walnut in upward thrust. Scientists call this molecule vibration, occurring when atoms in a molecule are in constant motion.

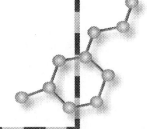

EGG POWER

Purpose
To demonstrate the strength of eggshells.

Curriculum
Geometric shapes

Requirements
Time: 3 minutes   *Difficulty Level:* 3

Materials
- two uncooked eggs
- masking tape
- scissors
- several books

Directions
1. Carefully crack open the two uncooked eggs in half so that you have four eggshell halves.
2. Clean out the eggshell halves. Wrap a piece of masking tape around the middle of each empty eggshell half. The tape should cover the entire edge of the eggshell, making a straight edge.
3. With the scissors, trim off the excess shell so that each one has a straight-edged bottom.
4. Lay out the four eggshells (dome up) so that they form a square.
5. Now, carefully lay your book face down on the four eggshells. Continue to carefully stack books on top of one another until the shells crack.
6. Discuss why the eggshells can hold this amount of weight.

Safety Note: Use caution when trimming the eggshells with the scissors.

Explanation
Eggshells can support a good deal of weight, so they should not crack right away. The secret of their strength is their shape. In this experiment, the weight is evenly distributed among all four eggshell halves. The weight is carried down along the arches (the curved tops of the egg) to the base of the square.

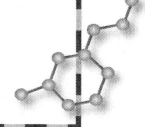

INSTANT MOUSSE

Purpose

To demonstrate how a polymer can be made from common food products.

Curriculum

Chemical reactions and gas formations

Requirements

Time: 5 minutes   *Difficulty Level:* 3

Materials

- two eggs
- water
- baking soda
- plastic cup
- crystallized citric acid (available at supermarkets)

Directions

1. Separate egg whites from yolks, discarding the yolks.
2. In a cup, mix together equal amounts of egg whites and water.
3. Add a generous amount of baking soda to the mixture of egg whites and water, and observe the reaction.
4. Sprinkle the crystallized citric acid over the mixture and stir together.
5. Observe the reaction that begins while mixing the citric acid into your mixture.
6. Demonstrate the thickness of the mousse you've created to your students by turning your cup upside down.
7. Discuss the reaction and the outcome.

Safety Note: Caution students not to eat this mousse because uncooked eggs can harbor salmonella bacteria.

Explanation

This experiment is an example of a chemical reaction that takes place every day in the kitchen. The baking soda releases carbon dioxide, which causes the egg white-and-water combination to inflate. The citric acid neutralizes the baking soda and acts as a thickener.

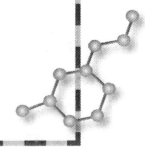

I SCREAM, YOU SCREAM, WE ALL SCREAM FOR ICE CREAM

Purpose

To demonstrate a change in energy matter.

Curriculum

Physical and phase changes

Requirements

Time: 20 minutes   *Difficulty Level:* 4

Materials

- 1 gallon-size plastic freezer bag
- 1 pint-size freezer bag
- ½ cup milk
- ½ teaspoon vanilla
- crushed ice
- 6 tablespoons of salt
- 1 tablespoon sugar

Directions

1. Place the crushed ice in the gallon freezer bag, filling it halfway.
2. Add the salt to the gallon-size bag and shake it, mixing the salt and ice together.
3. Seal the bag while squeezing out the excess air. Set aside.
4. Pour the milk, vanilla, and sugar into the small freezer bag, and seal the bag while squeezing out the air.
5. Place the sealed, smaller bag into the gallon-size bag.
6. Shake the bags for about 5–10 minutes until the mixture reaches a thick appearance like soft-serve ice cream.
7. Open the large bag and remove the small ice cream bag. Enjoy your homemade ice cream.
8. After enjoying the treat, discuss the physical changes that took place and how each ingredient affected the final outcome.

Safety Note: Because your students will no doubt want to eat their ice cream, advise them to use clean equipment and fresh ingredients for this activity.

Explanation

Several physical changes will take place during this experiment. The ice and salt will melt to liquid and absorb heat energy from the liquid milk mixture (which was warmer). This, in turn, causes the milk mixture to cool. As energy (heat) was being removed, the liquid will turn into a solid. Observing the freezing process in this activity helps visualize the principle that heat energy always flows into cooler materials.

Variations

Use whole, low-fat, and no-fat milk varieties for this activity and compare end results in terms of consistency (creaminess).

YEAST BEASTS

Purpose

To observe how yeast makes its own food.

Curriculum

Gas formation of food products

Requirements

Time: 25 minutes   *Difficulty Level:* 4

Materials

- two Ziploc® plastic sandwich bags
- two packets of dried baking yeast
- 1 teaspoon of granular sugar
- warm water
- measuring cup
- permanent marker

Directions

1. Label the plastic bags "Sugar" and "No sugar."
2. Pour one packet of yeast into each of the bags.
3. Pour the sugar into only the bag labeled "Sugar."
4. Pour ¼ cup of warm water into each bag.
5. Squeeze air from bags and carefully seal.
6. Gently shake the bags for about 1 minute.
7. After shaking the bags, let them sit for about 20 minutes. Check the bags about every 5 minutes.
8. Compare and contrast the bags after the 20 minutes have passed.

Explanation

Sugar is a food product, and therefore will cause the yeast to "grow." As it grows, it produces new yeast plants. In the process, the yeast gives off alcohol and carbon dioxide gas. This gas caused the bag to expand. Just adding water is not enough to make it grow. Yeast is a living body (fungus) and needs energy (sugar/food) to grow.

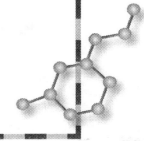

Kitchen Science

About the Author

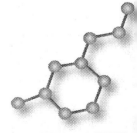

Phil Parratore has been an advocate of hands-on science for gifted students for more than three decades. He has a real passion for getting children and adults involved with science education. His philosophy is very simple: Gifted children learn best by active participation in the understanding of abstract concepts.

As a retired middle school math and science teacher for regular education, as well as gifted students, Phil has served as a science consultant to numerous school districts throughout the United States. Phil holds master's degrees in school administration and secondary education. At the university graduate level, he has trained more than 5,000 teachers in the art of hands-on science. Phil had a cable TV show for children called "The Wacky Science Show" that showcased many of the activities used in this book. This is Phil's 16th hands-on science book for children and educators.